USING CALCULATORS
For Business Problems

◆

THIRD EDITION

GARY BERG, Ph.D.

Dean, College of Business
Western International University
Phoenix, Arizona

LEO GAFNEY, Ed.D.

Business Curriculum Advisor,
Author, and Educational Consultant
Lakeville, Connecticut

PARADIGM

Developmental Editor: Leslie Joseph
Copy Editor: Roberta Mantis
Text Design: Mori Studio
Cover Design: Pam Belding

ACKNOWLEDGEMENTS

We wish to thank the following instructors and technical experts who contributed to this book:

Debra Housel
Educational Opportunity Center
Rochester, NY

Gilbert J. Ribera
Chabot College
Hayward, CA

E. Jean Jillson
Laramie County Community College
Laramie, WY

Mary Beth Williams
Herzing Institute
Birmingham, AL

Library of Congress Cataloging-in-Publication Data

Berg, Gary A., 1944-
    Using calculators for business problems / Gary A. Berg,
Leo Gafney. — 3rd ed.
        p. cm.
    Includes index.
    ISBN 1-56118-577-9
    1. Calculators—Problems, exercises, etc. 2. Business mathematics—Problems,
exercises, etc. I. Gafney, Leo. II. Title.
HF5688.B45 1993
650'.01'513—dc20
                                     92-43112
                                     CIP

CONTENTS

INTRODUCTION

Like all Paradigm products, this text develops skills and concepts for the workplace. Proficiency in the touch system for the calculator, mastery of basic math skills, and familiarity with business concepts will prepare you for a productive job and satisfying career.

Using the touch system for the calculator, you will be five or ten times faster than someone who does not use it. This increased speed means increased productivity, and employers want greater productivity because this leads, in turn, to increased profits. So after you master the touch system for the calculator, you will have a better chance of finding and keeping a job than if you had not developed such mastery.

Mathematical skills are needed in clerical work, sales and marketing, product development, and management. In fact, it is difficult to think of an area of office work or business that does not require mathematics.

An understanding of basic business concepts will enhance your value. When you understand the goals and procedures of your company or business, you will be able to take on increased responsibilities.

This text will help you become productive in your learning and in your future work. As you study this text and as you work with the calculator, pay attention to how each skill and each idea is really used, Good luck.

THE TOUCH SYSTEM: ADDITION BY ROWS AND COLUMNS

OBJECTIVES

After completing this lesson you will be able to:

- Locate and use the number keys using the touch system.
- Use the touch system on the numeric keypad to perform addition of one row or column at a time.

THE CALCULATOR

The calculator is one of the most frequently used tools in modern business. But a calculator is no better than the person using it. Become proficient in all the operations available on your calculator, and you help both yourself and your business.

All business calculators contain the basic function keys with which you add, subtract, multiply, and divide. Other common features are discussed and explained in lessons that follow. In addition to the shared features, different kinds of electronic calculators contain features designed for specific purposes. For example, printing calculators (see Figure 1.1) give you a printed record of all the numbers and operations that you enter. Standard business calculators (see Figure 1.2) are usually kept in a fixed position on a person's desk and have large keys for ease of use. Other types of calculators include the hand-held business-type pocket calculator (see Figure 1.3). Many computers contain an electronic keypad that works as a calculator when used in conjunction with the appropriate software.

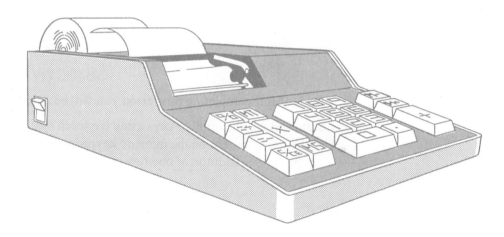

Figure 1.1   Printing calculator

Figure 1.2   Standard business calculator

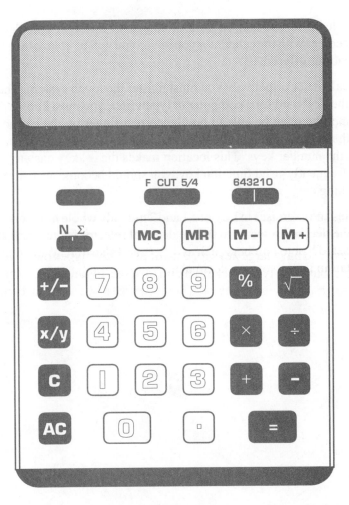

Figure 1.3   Hand-held business-type pocket calculator

Figure 1.4   Computer electronic keypad

You should learn to use and be comfortable with different calculators. Read the manual that comes with the calculator you use so you will be able to take full advantage of all the features offered.

To use the calculator effectively you must master the touch system. That means, just as in using the keyboard for a computer or typewriter, you must know where each key is located and you must be able to put the correct finger on the correct key without looking at the keypad. On most business calculators, the $+$ key is a large bar just to the right of the number keys. This location makes the $+$ key easy to reach. Since it is the most frequently-used function key, you should become accustomed to using it without looking.

The examples and exercises in Lessons 1 and 2 use only whole numbers. For these you should set the decimal selector to 0. The decimal selector is the small sliding switch that can be set to F or to numbers such as 4, 2, 0, and also to A. We discuss this feature in more detail in the lessons on decimals.

THE NUMERIC KEYPAD

A numeric keypad is shown in Figure 1.5. Correct finger position is shown in Figure 1.6. You will lightly rest the index, middle, and ring fingers of your right hand on the "home row," which is made up of numbers 4, 5, and 6. The thumb rests on the $\boxed{0}$ key. Many calculators have a raised dot on the $\boxed{5}$ key. The feel of this dot tells your middle finger that you are on the home row and that your fingers are positioned correctly.

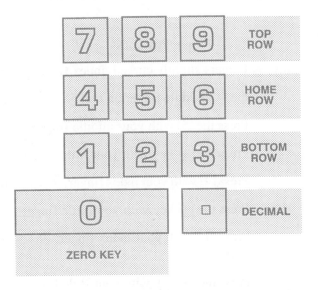

Figure 1.5   Numeric Keypad

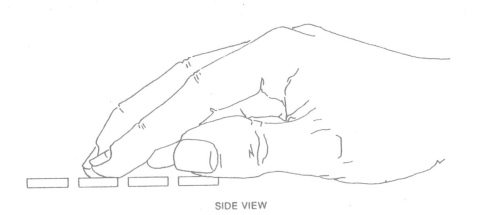

SIDE VIEW

Figure 1.6   Home-row keys

Each finger controls the keys that are on the home row and those directly above and below home row position. Thus the index finger controls the 1, 4, and 7; the middle finger, the 2, 5, and 8; and the ring finger, the 3, 6, and 9. Many calculators also have a 00 key. When working with amounts of money, you press this key instead of pressing the 0 key twice.

The only way to become proficient in the touch system is through practice. The remainder of this lesson is devoted to drills that will help you develop mastery of the touch system. You will practice the touch system one row at a time and one column at a time.

Note the following vocabulary. *Addends* are numbers that are added. The *sum* is the result of adding two or more numbers.

DEMONSTRATION EXAMPLE

On your calculator, find the sum for: 5 + 46 + 78 + 23. Follow the steps shown below:

		Finger Positions
Enter	Display	Fingers slightly curved, index finger resting lightly on the 4, middle finger on the 5, ring finger on the 6.
5		Press the 5 with your middle finger.
	5	Press the + key with your little finger.
46		Press 4 with your index finger; 6 with your ring finger.
	51	Press the + key with your little finger.
78		Press 7 with your index finger; 8 with your middle finger.
	129	Press the + key with your little finger.
23		Press 2 with your middle finger; 3 with your ring finger.
	152	Press the + key with your little finger.
	152	Press T or * to find the total; use a tape or read the screen.

▶ Place your index, middle, and ring fingers on the home row (4-5-6). Enter each set of digits, then press the ⊞ key. At the end of the problem press the ⊤ or ⁎ key, and record the answer on the answer tab. Work digits slowly at first; then speed up. Try to move from watching the keypad to inputting the numbers by touch.

Emphasizing 4-5-6

1.	456	2.	645	3.	465	4.	654	5.	546
	654		546		564		456		645

6.	564	7.	456	8.	645	9.	465	10.	564
	465		654		546		564		465

Emphasizing 4 with double numbers

11.	444	12.	445	13.	455	14.	446	15.	466
	455		446		466		444		445
	466		444		445		455		446

16.	455	17.	446	18.	466	19.	444	20.	445
	466		444		445		455		446
	445		455		446		466		444

Emphasizing 5 with double numbers

21.	555	22.	556	23.	544	24.	566	25.	554
	544		566		554		555		556
	554		555		556		544		566

26.	544	27.	566	28.	554	29.	555	30.	556
	554		555		556		544		566
	556		544		566		554		555

Emphasizing 6 with double numbers

31.	666	32.	665	33.	655	34.	664	35.	644
	655		664		644		666		665
	644		666		665		655		664

36.	655	37.	644	38.	644	39.	666	40.	665
	644		666		665		655		664
	665		655		664		644		666

1. _____
2. _____
3. _____
4. _____
5. _____
6. _____
7. _____
8. _____
9. _____
10. _____
11. _____
12. _____
13. _____
14. _____
15. _____
16. _____
17. _____
18. _____
19. _____
20. _____
21. _____
22. _____
23. _____
24. _____
25. _____
26. _____
27. _____
28. _____
29. _____
30. _____
31. _____
32. _____
33. _____
34. _____
35. _____
36. _____
37. _____
38. _____
39. _____
40. _____

Name_____

2. 7-8-9 KEYS

▶ Locate the 7-8-9 keys. Place your index, middle, and ring fingers on the home row (4-5-6). Find each sum and write your answer on the answer tab. Try to move from watching the keypad to inputting the numbers by touch.

Emphasizing 7-8-9

1. 789	2. 879	3. 897	4. 987	5. 798
987	798	978	789	879

6. 978	7. 789	8. 879	9. 897	10. 987
897	987	798	798	789

Emphasizing 7 with double numbers

11. 777	12. 788	13. 778	14. 799	15. 787
778	799	779	777	788
779	777	788	778	799

16. 779	17. 777	18. 788	19. 778	20. 799
788	778	799	777	777
778	799	779	779	788

Emphasizing 8 with double numbers

21. 888	22. 877	23. 889	24. 899	25. 887
889	899	887	888	877
887	888	877	889	899

26. 889	27. 899	28. 887	29. 888	30. 877
887	888	877	889	899
877	889	899	887	888

Emphasizing 9 with double numbers

31. 999	32. 988	33. 998	34. 977	35. 997
998	977	997	999	988
997	999	988	998	977

36. 977	37. 997	38. 999	39. 988	40. 998
998	977	997	999	988
999	988	998	977	997

Answer tab:

1. _____
2. _____
3. _____
4. _____
5. _____
6. _____
7. _____
8. _____
9. _____
10. _____
11. _____
12. _____
13. _____
14. _____
15. _____
16. _____
17. _____
18. _____
19. _____
20. _____
21. _____
22. _____
23. _____
24. _____
25. _____
26. _____
27. _____
28. _____
29. _____
30. _____
31. _____
32. _____
33. _____
34. _____
35. _____
36. _____
37. _____
38. _____
39. _____
40. _____

Name _____

▶ Locate the 1-2-3 keys. Place your index, middle, and ring fingers on the home row (4-5-6). Find each sum and write your answer on the answer tab. Try to move from watching the keypad to inputting the numbers by touch.

Emphasizing 1-2-3

1. 123 321	2. 231 312	3. 132 213	4. 321 123	5. 312 231
6. 213 132	7. 123 321	8. 132 312	9. 213 123	10. 231 312

Emphasizing 3 with double numbers

11. 333 332 311	12. 322 321 333	13. 332 311 322	14. 321 333 332	15. 311 322 321
16. 311 332 322	17. 333 321 332	18. 321 311 322	19. 332 333 311	20. 333 321 322

Emphasizing 2 with double numbers

21. 222 221 223	22. 211 233 222	23. 221 223 211	24. 233 222 221	25. 223 211 233
26. 223 211 221	27. 222 221 233	28. 211 233 223	29. 221 223 222	30. 233 222 211

Emphasizing 1 with double numbers

31. 111 112 113	32. 122 133 111	33. 112 113 122	34. 133 111 112	35. 113 122 133
36. 113 122 112	37. 111 133 112	38. 122 113 133	39. 112 113 111	40. 133 122 111

Addition by Rows and Columns • 9

1. _____
2. _____
3. _____
4. _____
5. _____
6. _____
7. _____
8. _____
9. _____
10. _____
11. _____
12. _____
13. _____
14. _____
15. _____
16. _____
17. _____
18. _____
19. _____
20. _____
21. _____
22. _____
23. _____
24. _____
25. _____
26. _____
27. _____
28. _____
29. _____
30. _____
31. _____
32. _____
33. _____
34. _____
35. _____
36. _____
37. _____
38. _____
39. _____
40. _____

Name_____

EXERCISE 4: 8-5-2 KEYS

▶ Locate the 8-5-2 keys. Place your index, middle, and ring fingers on the home row (4-5-6). Find each sum and write your answer on the answer tab. Try to move from watching the keypad to inputting the numbers by touch.

Emphasizing 8-5-2

1. 852	2. 528	3. 285	4. 258	5. 825
258	825	582	852	528

6. 582	7. 852	8. 258	9. 285	10. 852
285	258	528	582	258

Emphasizing 8 with double numbers

11. 888	12. 822	13. 882	14. 855	15. 885
882	855	885	888	822
885	888	822	882	855

16. 855	17. 882	18. 822	19. 888	20. 885
822	888	885	855	822
885	855	882	822	888

Emphasizing 5 with double numbers

21. 555	22. 588	23. 558	24. 522	25. 552
558	522	552	555	588
552	555	588	558	522

26. 522	27. 558	28. 588	29. 555	30. 552
588	555	552	522	558
552	522	558	588	555

Emphasizing 2 with double numbers

31. 222	32. 288	33. 225	34. 255	35. 228
225	255	228	222	288
228	222	288	225	255

36. 255	37. 225	38. 288	39. 222	40. 228
288	222	228	255	225
228	255	225	288	222

Answer tab:

1. _____
2. _____
3. _____
4. _____
5. _____
6. _____
7. _____
8. _____
9. _____
10. _____
11. _____
12. _____
13. _____
14. _____
15. _____
16. _____
17. _____
18. _____
19. _____
20. _____
21. _____
22. _____
23. _____
24. _____
25. _____
26. _____
27. _____
28. _____
29. _____
30. _____
31. _____
32. _____
33. _____
34. _____
35. _____
36. _____
37. _____
38. _____
39. _____
40. _____

▶ Locate the 7-4-1 keys. Place your index, middle, and ring fingers on the home row (4-5-6). Find each sum and write your answer on the answer tab. Try to move from watching the keypad to inputting the numbers by touch.

Emphasizing 7-4-1

1. 741	2. 147	3. 714	4. 471	5. 417
471	417	174	741	147

6. 174	7. 471	8. 147	9. 714	10. 741
714	741	417	174	471

Emphasizing 1 with double numbers

11. 111	12. 177	13. 117	14. 144	15. 114
117	144	114	111	177
114	111	177	117	144

16. 114	17. 117	18. 117	19. 177	20. 144
117	111	114	144	111
177	144	111	114	177

Emphasizing 7 with double numbers

21. 777	22. 711	23. 774	24. 744	25. 771
774	744	771	777	711
771	777	711	774	744

26. 771	27. 777	28. 744	29. 744	30. 774
711	774	711	711	771
774	744	771	777	777

Emphasizing 4 with double numbers

31. 444	32. 477	33. 447	34. 411	35. 441
447	411	441	444	477
441	444	477	447	411

36. 441	37. 444	38. 411	39. 477	40. 447
477	411	477	411	444
447	447	441	444	441

1. _____
2. _____
3. _____
4. _____
5. _____
6. _____
7. _____
8. _____
9. _____
10. _____
11. _____
12. _____
13. _____
14. _____
15. _____
16. _____
17. _____
18. _____
19. _____
20. _____
21. _____
22. _____
23. _____
24. _____
25. _____
26. _____
27. _____
28. _____
29. _____
30. _____
31. _____
32. _____
33. _____
34. _____
35. _____
36. _____
37. _____
38. _____
39. _____
40. _____

Name _____

EXERCISE 6: 9-6-3 KEYS

▶ Locate the 9-6-3 keys. Place your index, middle, and ring fingers on the home row (4-5-6). Find each sum and write your answer on the answer tab. Try to move from watching the keypad to inputting the numbers by touch.

Emphasizing 9-6-3

1. 963	2. 396	3. 639	4. 369	5. 396
369	693	936	963	693

6. 936	7. 693	8. 639	9. 963	10. 936
639	369	396	369	963

Emphasizing 9 with double numbers

11. 999	12. 933	13. 996	14. 966	15. 993
996	966	993	999	933
993	999	933	996	966

16. 966	17. 996	18. 933	19. 999	20. 993
933	999	996	966	933
993	966	993	933	996

Emphasizing 6 with double numbers

21. 666	22. 633	23. 669	24. 699	25. 663
669	699	663	666	633
663	666	633	669	699

26. 699	27. 669	28. 633	29. 666	30. 663
633	666	663	699	669
663	699	669	633	666

Emphasizing 3 with double numbers

31. 333	32. 399	33. 336	34. 366	35. 339
336	366	339	333	399
339	333	399	336	366

36. 366	37. 336	38. 399	39. 333	40. 339
399	333	339	366	336
339	366	336	399	333

1. _____
2. _____
3. _____
4. _____
5. _____
6. _____
7. _____
8. _____
9. _____
10. _____
11. _____
12. _____
13. _____
14. _____
15. _____
16. _____
17. _____
18. _____
19. _____
20. _____
21. _____
22. _____
23. _____
24. _____
25. _____
26. _____
27. _____
28. _____
29. _____
30. _____
31. _____
32. _____
33. _____
34. _____
35. _____
36. _____
37. _____
38. _____
39. _____
40. _____

Name _____

Lesson 1

TOUCH DRILL FOR SPEED DEVELOPMENT

▶ The following exercises review everything that you have covered in this lesson. Find each sum and write your answers on the tab. Try to work without looking at the calculator keys. Remember to return you fingers to the home row after each entry. Record the total number of minutes and seconds it takes to complete these exercises on the line provided.

1.	64 655	2.	897 98	3.	23 112	4.	789 879	5.	13 22

6.	89 798	7.	936 639	8.	822 258	9.	74 147	10.	312 132

11.	54 66 56	12.	778 798 987	13.	465 55 654	14.	788 897 89	15.	312 23 231

16.	966 996 633 936 396	17.	552 858 282 825 285	18.	471 771 474 741 147	19.	825 558 255 528 852	20.	399 39 693 96 366

21.	556 654 66 644 565	22.	879 98 879 787 989	23.	311 31 322 313 232	24.	79 789 877 797 878	25.	213 33 312 121 323

26.	47 141 17 474 741	27.	25 585 252 285 528	28.	336 969 63 396 693	29.	525 52 282 582 285	30.	717 747 414 47 717

TIME _____

TOUCH DRILL FOR SPEED DEVELOPMENT

1. _____
2. _____
3. _____
4. _____
5. _____
6. _____
7. _____
8. _____
9. _____
10. _____
11. _____
12. _____
13. _____
14. _____
15. _____
16. _____
17. _____
18. _____
19. _____
20. _____
21. _____
22. _____
23. _____
24. _____
25. _____
26. _____
27. _____
28. _____
29. _____
30. _____

Name _____

Lesson 1

APPLY YOUR SKILLS

1. _____

2. _____

3. _____

4. _____

5. _____

6. _____

7. _____

8. _____

9. _____

▶ At the Globe Department Store, the owners and managers are interested not only in the amount of sales but also in the numbers of people entering the store and visiting the different departments. The following lists show the number of customers entering different departments. Find the totals for each department and write your answers on the blank lines following the word "Total."

1. Electronics		2. Grocery		3. Lamps	
Mon	465	Mon	88	Mon	312
Tues	54	Tues	887	Tues	221
Wed	645	Wed	99	Wed	133
Thurs	446	Thurs	978	Thurs	211
Fri	665	Fri	897	Fri	321
Total _____		Total _____		Total _____	

4. Cafeteria		5. Bookstore		6. Furniture	
Mon	528	Mon	96	Mon	744
Tues	852	Tues	663	Tues	471
Wed	85	Wed	396	Wed	77
Thurs	228	Thurs	933	Thurs	141
Fri	585	Fri	363	Fri	477
Total _____		Total _____		Total _____	

7. Jewelry		8. Men's Clothes		9. Hardware	
Mon	96	Mon	665	Mon	141
Tues	366	Tues	556	Tues	471
Wed	693	Wed	65	Wed	717
Thurs	966	Thurs	465	Thurs	747
Fri	633	Fri	545	Fri	411
Total _____		Total _____		Total _____	

CHECK YOUR PROGRESS

▶ Place your fingers on the home row. Find each sum and write your answers on the answer tab. Remember to return your fingers to the home row after each entry.

1.	564	2.	879	3.	123	4.	779	5.	213
	645		798		331		897		112

6.	714	7.	825	8.	936	9.	558	10.	774
	147		285		663		852		174

11.	654	12.	556	13.	132	14.	112	15.	978
	464		465		212		213		787
	546		664		221		321		978

16.	936	17.	852	18.	771	19.	144	20.	369
	396		558		741		474		339
	693		882		174		711		633

1. _____
2. _____
3. _____
4. _____
5. _____
6. _____
7. _____
8. _____
9. _____
10. _____
11. _____
12. _____
13. _____
14. _____
15. _____
16. _____
17. _____
18. _____
19. _____
20. _____

Name_____

Lesson 1
MASTERY CHECKPOINT

1. _____
2. _____
3. _____
4. _____
5. _____
6. _____
7. _____
8. _____
9. _____
10. _____
11. _____
12. _____
13. _____
14. _____
15. _____
16. _____
17. _____
18. _____
19. _____
20. _____

▶ Place your fingers on the home row. Find each sum and write your answers on the answer tab. Remember to return your fingers to the home row after each entry.

1. 566	2. 779	3. 321	4. 879	5. 113
654	898	131	899	133

6. 742	7. 525	8. 936	9. 528	10. 714
141	582	963	252	147

11. 664	12. 546	13. 132	14. 132	15. 979
446	465	312	213	778
546	654	212	322	978

16. 936	17. 822	18. 741	19. 744	20. 339
366	588	441	417	369
633	852	474	771	933

THE TOUCH SYSTEM: ADDITION AND SUBTRACTION OF WHOLE NUMBERS

OBJECTIVES

After completing this lesson you will be able to:

- Use the numeric keypad to add whole numbers.
- Use the numeric keypad to subtract whole numbers.
- Use the $+$ and $-$ keys with speed and accuracy.

ADDING WHOLE NUMBERS

In Lesson 1 you may have looked at the keys fairly often. In this lesson, make an effort to use the touch system without looking at the keys.

Figure 2.1 shows the keypad with certain keys highlighted. The drills in this lesson work on these different groups of keys so that you will gradually develop a sense of the entire keypad.

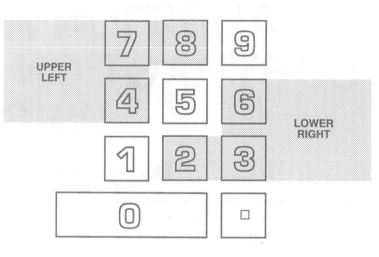

Figure 2.1   Keys to be worked in Lesson 2

DEMONSTRATION EXAMPLE

Add: 6 + 26 + 362

Add	Fingers slightly curved, index finger resting lightly on the $\boxed{4}$, middle finger on the $\boxed{5}$, ring finger on the $\boxed{6}$.
6	Press the $\boxed{6}$ with your ring finger.
	Press the $\boxed{+}$ key with your little finger.
26	Press $\boxed{2}$ with your middle finger; $\boxed{6}$ with your ring finger. Add.
362	Press $\boxed{3}$ with your ring finger; $\boxed{6}$ with your ring finger; $\boxed{2}$ with your middle finger. Add.
394	Read the total from the display or press $\boxed{T}$ or $\boxed{*}$ for the total on a tape.

▶ Find each sum. Write your answer on the answer tab. Remember to return your fingers to the home row after each entry. Use the touch system for the function keys as well as for the number keys.

Emphasizing 7-5-3

1. 753	2. 537	3. 375	4. 357	5. 735
357	735	573	537	375

6. 583	7. 538	8. 358	9. 385	10. 853
375	537	753	573	357

Emphasizing 7 with double numbers

11. 777	12. 755	13. 773	14. 733	15. 773
775	733	775	777	755
773	777	755	775	733

16. 733	17. 775	18. 755	19. 777	20. 773
755	777	773	733	775
773	733	775	755	777

Emphasizing 5 with double numbers

21. 555	22. 533	23. 557	24. 577	25. 553
557	577	553	555	533
553	555	533	557	577

26. 577	27. 557	28. 533	29. 555	30. 553
533	555	553	577	557
553	577	557	533	555

Emphasizing 3 with double numbers

31. 333	32. 355	33. 335	34. 377	35. 337
335	377	337	333	355
337	333	355	335	377

36. 377	37. 335	38. 355	39. 333	40. 335
355	333	337	377	335
337	377	335	355	333

1. _____
2. _____
3. _____
4. _____
5. _____
6. _____
7. _____
8. _____
9. _____
10. _____
11. _____
12. _____
13. _____
14. _____
15. _____
16. _____
17. _____
18. _____
19. _____
20. _____
21. _____
22. _____
23. _____
24. _____
25. _____
26. _____
27. _____
28. _____
29. _____
30. _____
31. _____
32. _____
33. _____
34. _____
35. _____
36. _____
37. _____
38. _____
39. _____
40. _____

Name _____

1. _____
2. _____
3. _____
4. _____
5. _____
6. _____
7. _____
8. _____
9. _____
10. _____
11. _____
12. _____
13. _____
14. _____
15. _____
16. _____
17. _____
18. _____
19. _____
20. _____
21. _____
22. _____
23. _____
24. _____
25. _____
26. _____
27. _____
28. _____
29. _____
30. _____
31. _____
32. _____
33. _____
34. _____
35. _____
36. _____
37. _____
38. _____
39. _____
40. _____

EXERCISE 2: 8-6-9 KEYS

▶ Find each sum. Write your answer on the answer tab. Remember to return your fingers to the home row after each entry. Use the touch system for the function keys, ⊞ and ═, as well as for the number keys.

Emphasizing 8-6-9

1. 869	2. 689	3. 986	4. 968	5. 896
968	896	698	689	986

6. 698	7. 896	8. 968	9. 698	10. 968
968	689	869	689	986

Emphasizing 8 with double numbers

11. 888	12. 899	13. 889	14. 888	15. 899
886	866	899	886	866
889	888	866	889	888

16. 866	17. 886	18. 899	19. 888	20. 889
899	888	889	866	886
889	866	886	899	888

Emphasizing 9 with double numbers

21. 999	22. 988	23. 996	24. 966	25. 998
996	966	998	999	988
998	999	988	996	966

26. 966	27. 996	28. 988	29. 999	30. 998
988	999	998	966	996
998	966	996	988	999

Emphasizing 6 with double numbers

31. 666	32. 688	33. 669	34. 699	35. 668
669	699	668	666	688
669	666	688	669	699

36. 699	37. 669	38. 688	39. 666	40. 668
699	666	668	699	669
668	699	669	688	666

▶ Find each sum. Write your answer on the answer tab. Remember to return your fingers to the home row after each entry. Use the touch system for the function keys, $+$ and $=$, as well as for the number keys.

Emphasizing 4-2-1

1. 421	2. 241	3. 412	4. 124	5. 142
124	142	214	421	241

6. 214	7. 142	8. 124	9. 241	10. 214
412	241	421	412	124

Emphasizing 4 with double numbers

11. 444	12. 411	13. 442	14. 422	15. 441
442	422	441	444	411
441	444	411	442	422

16. 422	17. 442	18. 411	19. 444	20. 441
411	444	441	422	442
441	422	442	411	444

Emphasizing 2 with double numbers

21. 222	22. 211	23. 224	24. 244	25. 221
224	244	221	222	211
221	222	211	224	244

26. 244	27. 224	28. 211	29. 222	30. 221
211	222	221	244	224
221	244	224	211	222

Emphasizing 1 with double numbers

31. 111	32. 122	33. 114	34. 144	35. 112
114	144	112	111	122
112	111	122	114	144

36. 144	37. 114	38. 122	39. 111	40. 112
122	111	112	144	114
112	144	114	122	111

1. _____
2. _____
3. _____
4. _____
5. _____
6. _____
7. _____
8. _____
9. _____
10. _____
11. _____
12. _____
13. _____
14. _____
15. _____
16. _____
17. _____
18. _____
19. _____
20. _____
21. _____
22. _____
23. _____
24. _____
25. _____
26. _____
27. _____
28. _____
29. _____
30. _____
31. _____
32. _____
33. _____
34. _____
35. _____
36. _____
37. _____
38. _____
39. _____
40. _____

Name _____

1. _____
2. _____
3. _____
4. _____
5. _____
6. _____
7. _____
8. _____
9. _____
10. _____
11. _____
12. _____
13. _____
14. _____
15. _____
16. _____
17. _____
18. _____
19. _____
20. _____
21. _____
22. _____
23. _____
24. _____
25. _____
26. _____
27. _____
28. _____
29. _____
30. _____
31. _____
32. _____
33. _____
34. _____
35. _____
36. _____
37. _____
38. _____
39. _____
40. _____

EXERCISE 4: 9-5-1 KEYS

▶ Find each sum. Write your answer on the answer tab. Remember to return your fingers to the home row after each entry. Use the touch system for the function keys, $+$ and $=$, as well as for the number keys.

Emphasizing 9-5-1

1. 951	2. 591	3. 195	4. 159	5. 519
159	519	915	591	195

6. 915	7. 519	8. 159	9. 519	10. 159
195	591	951	591	195

Emphasizing 9 with double numbers

11. 999	12. 911	13. 991	14. 955	15. 995
991	955	995	999	911
995	999	911	991	955

16. 955	17. 991	18. 911	19. 999	20. 995
911	999	995	955	991
995	955	991	911	999

Emphasizing 5 with double numbers

21. 555	22. 599	23. 559	24. 511	25. 551
559	511	551	555	599
551	555	599	559	511

26. 511	27. 559	28. 599	29. 555	30. 551
599	555	551	511	559
551	511	559	599	555

Emphasizing 1 with double numbers

31. 111	32. 199	33. 119	34. 155	35. 115
119	155	115	111	199
115	111	199	119	155

36. 155	37. 119	38. 199	39. 111	40. 115
199	111	115	155	119
115	155	119	199	111

Name _____

▶ Find each sum. Write your answer on the answer tab. Remember to return your fingers to the home row after each entry. Use the touch system for the function keys, ⊞ and ⊟, as well as for the number keys.

Emphasizing 7-8-4

1. 784	2. 874	3. 847	4. 487	5. 748
487	748	478	874	847

6. 478	7. 748	8. 487	9. 784	10. 487
847	874	487	478	847

Emphasizing 7 with double numbers

11. 777	12. 744	13. 774	14. 788	15. 778
774	788	778	777	744
778	777	744	774	788

16. 788	17. 774	18. 744	19. 777	20. 778
744	777	778	788	774
778	788	774	744	777

Emphasizing 8 with double numbers

21. 888	22. 844	23. 884	24. 877	25. 887
884	844	887	888	844
887	888	844	884	877

26. 877	27. 884	28. 844	29. 888	30. 887
844	888	887	877	884
887	877	884	844	888

Emphasizing 4 with double numbers

31. 444	32. 488	33. 448	34. 477	35. 447
448	477	447	444	488
447	444	488	448	477

36. 477	37. 448	38. 488	39. 444	40. 447
488	444	447	477	488
447	477	448	488	444

1. _____
2. _____
3. _____
4. _____
5. _____
6. _____
7. _____
8. _____
9. _____
10. _____
11. _____
12. _____
13. _____
14. _____
15. _____
16. _____
17. _____
18. _____
19. _____
20. _____
21. _____
22. _____
23. _____
24. _____
25. _____
26. _____
27. _____
28. _____
29. _____
30. _____
31. _____
32. _____
33. _____
34. _____
35. _____
36. _____
37. _____
38. _____
39. _____
40. _____

Name _____

1. _____
2. _____
3. _____
4. _____
5. _____
6. _____
7. _____
8. _____
9. _____
10. _____
11. _____
12. _____
13. _____
14. _____
15. _____
16. _____
17. _____
18. _____
19. _____
20. _____
21. _____
22. _____
23. _____
24. _____
25. _____
26. _____
27. _____
28. _____
29. _____
30. _____
31. _____
32. _____
33. _____
34. _____
35. _____
36. _____
37. _____
38. _____
39. _____
40. _____

EXERCISE 6: 6-2-3 KEYS

▶ Find each sum. Write your answer on the answer tab. Remember to return your fingers to the home row after each entry. Use the touch system for the function keys, $+$ and $=$, as well as for the number keys.

Emphasizing 6-2-3

1. 623	2. 236	3. 362	4. 632	5. 326
326	632	263	362	236

6. 263	7. 632	8. 326	9. 623	10. 326
362	236	623	263	362

Emphasizing 6 with double numbers

11. 666	12. 622	13. 663	14. 633	15. 662
663	633	662	666	622
663	666	622	663	633

16. 633	17. 663	18. 622	19. 666	20. 662
622	666	662	633	663
662	633	663	622	666

Emphasizing 2 with double numbers

21. 222	22. 266	23. 223	24. 233	25. 226
223	233	226	222	266
226	222	266	223	233

26. 233	27. 223	28. 266	29. 222	30. 223
266	222	223	233	223
226	233	223	266	222

Emphasizing 3 with double numbers

31. 333	32. 322	33. 336	34. 366	35. 332
336	366	332	333	322
332	333	322	336	366

36. 366	37. 336	38. 322	39. 333	40. 332
322	333	332	366	336
332	366	336	322	333

SUBTRACTING WHOLE NUMBERS

On business calculators, the ☐ key is generally above or to the right of the ⊞ key. When using business calculators, you press ☐ after entering the number you are subtracting. A *difference* is the result of subtracting one number from another.

DEMONSTRATION EXAMPLE

Using your calculator, find the answer to the following:

526 + 217 – 278. Follow the steps shown below:

Enter	Display	
526		Press the ⑤ with your middle finger; ② with your middle finger; and ⑥ with your ring finger.
	526	Press ⊞ with your little finger.
217		Press ② with your middle finger; ① with your index finger; ⑦ with your index finger.
	743	Press ⊞ with your little finger.
278		Press ② with your ring finger; ⑦ with your index finger; ⑧ with your middle finger. Press ☐ with your little finger.
	465	Read the total from display or press ⊤ or ⁕ to find the total.

EXERCISE 7: SUBTRACTION

▶ Find the difference in each exercise below. Write your answers on the answer tab.

1. _____
2. _____
3. _____
4. _____
5. _____
6. _____
7. _____
8. _____
9. _____
10. _____
11. _____
12. _____
13. _____
14. _____
15. _____
16. _____
17. _____
18. _____
19. _____
20. _____
21. _____
22. _____
23. _____
24. _____
25. _____

1. 328	2. 583	3. 945	4. 264	5. 762
−274	−378	−741	−98	−599

6. 627	7. 297	8. 168	9. 851	10. 238
−531	−167	−97	−761	−136

11. 376	12. 765	13. 726	14. 687	15. 257
−218	−168	−591	−321	−256

16. 896	17. 412	18. 487	19. 623	20. 591
−688	−142	−478	−236	−519

21. 753	22. 874	23. 652	24. 456	25. 897
−213	−528	−254	−378	−778

Name _____

Lesson 2
TOUCH DRILL FOR SPEED DEVELOPMENT

▶ The exercises below include all the numbers covered in this lesson. Find each sum. Write your answers on the answer tab. Record the total number of minutes and seconds it takes to complete these exercises on the line provided.

1. 478	2. 124	3. 557	4. 195	5. 236
887	214	753	991	332

6. 122	7. 689	8. 787	9. 919	10. 575
421	968	878	515	373

11. 951	12. 424	13. 878	14. 262	15. 737
155	212	474	633	375
911	421	748	263	535
159	214	487	632	753
919	414	787	232	737

16. 232	17. 753	18. 124	19. 784	20. 159
323	373	421	884	119
622	575	414	747	995
326	375	221	878	195
632	735	442	774	111

21. 995	22. 753	23. 519	24. 424	25. 632
919	373	191	242	236
595	573	591	121	232
159	735	919	124	623
915	377	191	142	236

26. 236	27. 753	28. 744	29. 787	30. 519
636	373	117	784	151
262	757	871	848	195
263	357	178	487	591
623	735	817	878	919

TIME _____

TOUCH DRILL
FOR SPEED
DEVELOPMENT

1. _____
2. _____
3. _____
4. _____
5. _____
6. _____
7. _____
8. _____
9. _____
10. _____
11. _____
12. _____
13. _____
14. _____
15. _____
16. _____
17. _____
18. _____
19. _____
20. _____
21. _____
22. _____
23. _____
24. _____
25. _____
26. _____
27. _____
28. _____
29. _____
30. _____

Name _____

1. _____

2. _____

3. _____

4. _____

5. _____

6. _____

7. _____

8. _____

9. _____

Lesson 2
APPLY YOUR SKILLS

▶ The owners of Playland Amusement Park think they can improve their profits if they pay attention to the number of people going on the different rides and attractions. The following are the reports for one week. Find each sum and write your answers on the blank lines following the word "Total."

1. Ferris Wheel		2. Roller Coaster		3. Rocket	
Wed	896	Wed	124	Wed	159
Thurs	689	Thurs	424	Thurs	519
Fri	868	Fri	412	Fri	599
Sat	698	Sat	1,241	Sat	919
Sun	986	Sun	1,442	Sun	1,191
Total _____		Total _____		Total _____	

4. Giant Slide		5. Great Swings		6. Haunted House	
Wed	73	Wed	623	Wed	78
Thurs	357	Thurs	366	Thurs	477
Fri	537	Fri	633	Fri	747
Sat	737	Sat	363	Sat	748
Sun	753	Sun	632	Sun	874
Total _____		Total _____		Total _____	

7. Caterpillar		8. Bumper Cars		9. Carousel	
Wed	75	Wed	124	Wed	478
Thurs	375	Thurs	214	Thurs	747
Fri	573	Fri	421	Fri	878
Sat	737	Sat	1,214	Sat	487
Sun	755	Sun	1,421	Sun	874
Total _____		Total _____		Total _____	

Lesson 2
CHECK YOUR PROGRESS

▶ Place your fingers on the home row. Find each sum or difference and write your answers on the answer tab. Remember to return your fingers to the home row after each entry.

|---|---|---|---|---|
1. 698 889	2. 869 996	3. 757 733	4. 337 577	5. 753 537
6. 214 −142	7. 421 −244	8. 688 −668	9. 968 −869	10. 998 −966
11. 955 119 195	12. 191 595 915	13. 159 519 991	14. 114 214 421	15. 412 211 141
16. 236 326 663	17. 623 363 226	18. 784 747 474	19. 744 484 748	20. 159 119 995

1. _____
2. _____
3. _____
4. _____
5. _____
6. _____
7. _____
8. _____
9. _____
10. _____
11. _____
12. _____
13. _____
14. _____
15. _____
16. _____
17. _____
18. _____
19. _____
20. _____

Name _____

MASTERY CHECKPOINT

1. _____
2. _____
3. _____
4. _____
5. _____
6. _____
7. _____
8. _____
9. _____
10. _____
11. _____
12. _____
13. _____
14. _____
15. _____
16. _____
17. _____
18. _____
19. _____
20. _____

▶ Place your fingers on the home row. Find each sum or remainder and write your answers on the answer tab. Remember to return your fingers to the home row after each entry.

1. 668	2. 669	3. 557	4. 357	5. 353
689	886	733	533	737

6. 244	7. 441	8. 689	9. 986	10. 998
−242	−124	−598	−896	−896

11. 915	12. 591	13. 119	14. 124	15. 112
519	515	599	244	241
595	115	591	121	241

16. 266	17. 633	18. 744	19. 484	20. 119
236	263	887	784	159
263	236	874	878	195

CALCULATING WITH DECIMAL NUMBERS: ADDITION AND SUBTRACTION

OBJECTIVES

After completing this lesson you will be able to:

- Add and subtract decimal numbers.
- Use the decimal selector correctly.

USING THE DECIMAL SELECTOR

In business, you will often compute with decimal numbers. The decimal point separates the whole number part from the decimal part of a number. When adding decimals that are not amounts of money, it is important to enter the decimal point for each number. Business calculators have a decimal selector feature.

The decimal selector allows you to choose the number of decimal places to be retained and displayed in your answer. On a typical business calculator this feature will show, "F 4 2 0 A." These five settings work as follows:

F   The decimal point "floats." The display or tape will show as many places as possible. For example, a calculator with a 10-place display will show $2 \div 3 = 0.666666666$.

4   The calculator rounds to four decimal places. $2 \div 3 = 0.6667$

2   The calculator rounds to two decimal places. $2 \div 3 = 0.67$

0   The calculator rounds to whole numbers. $2 \div 3 = 1$

A   This represents the "Add mode." The calculator shows each entry as a number with two decimal places as soon as a function key is pressed. For example, when you enter: 4 5 6 + the calculator display or tape will show 4.56.

The decimal setting or a separate key is marked RO or 5/4. RO stands for Rounding. 5/4 means that the decimal rounds up if the digit after the rounding place is 5 or greater. If the digit after the rounding place is 4 or less, the digit in the rounding place is left unchanged.

In this lesson, you will begin using the 0 key. For this, you should use your thumb.

DEMONSTRATION EXAMPLE

Set your decimal selector at 2.

Add 3.78 + 9.045. Explain the answer.

$3.78 + 9.045 = 12.83$

The calculator rounded the answer to two places.

It rounded up because the number in the thousandths place was 5.

EXERCISE 1: 0 AND DECIMAL (.) KEYS

▶ Locate the ⬚0 and ⬚· keys. Place your index, middle, and ring fingers on the home row (4-5-6). Enter each set of digits, then press the ⬚+ key. At the end of the problem, press the ⬚= key and record the answer on the answer tab. Try to move from watching the keypad to inputting the numbers by touch.

Emphasizing the 0 and decimal (.).
▶ Set the decimal selector at 2.

1. 10	2. 40	3. 70	4. .01	5. .04
20	50	80	.02	.05
<u>30</u>	<u>60</u>	<u>90</u>	<u>.03</u>	<u>.06</u>

6. .07	7. 101	8. 104	9. 107	10. 10.1
.08	102	105	108	10.2
<u>.09</u>	<u>103</u>	<u>106</u>	<u>109</u>	<u>10.3</u>

Emphasizing the 0 and decimal (.) with the numerical keyboard.
▶ Set the decimal selector at 4.

11. 10.4	12. 10.7	13. 1.010	14. 1.040	15. 1.070
10.5	10.8	1.020	1.050	1.080
<u>10.7</u>	<u>10.9</u>	<u>1.030</u>	<u>1.060</u>	<u>1.090</u>

16. 2.010	17. 2.040	18. 2.070	19. 30.10	20. 30.40
2.020	2.050	2.080	30.20	30.50
<u>2.030</u>	<u>2.060</u>	<u>2.090</u>	<u>30.30</u>	<u>30.60</u>

21. 30.70	22. 40.10	23. 40.40	24. 40.70	25. 5.010
30.80	40.20	40.50	40.80	5.020
<u>30.90</u>	<u>40.30</u>	<u>40.60</u>	<u>40.90</u>	<u>5.030</u>

26. 5.040	27. 5.070	28. 6.010	29. 6.040	30. 6.070
5.050	5.080	6.020	6.050	6.080
<u>5.060</u>	<u>5.090</u>	<u>6.030</u>	<u>6.060</u>	<u>6.090</u>

31. .7010	32. .7040	33. .7070	34. .8010	35. .8050
.7020	.7050	.7080	.8020	.8050
<u>.7030</u>	<u>.7060</u>	<u>.7090</u>	<u>.8030</u>	<u>.8060</u>

36. .8070	37. 90.10	38. 90.40	39. 90.70	40. 1000
.8080	90.20	90.50	90.80	2000
<u>.8090</u>	<u>90.30</u>	<u>90.60</u>	<u>90.90</u>	<u>3000</u>

1. 0 AND DECIMAL (.) KEYS

1. _____
2. _____
3. _____
4. _____
5. _____
6. _____
7. _____
8. _____
9. _____
10. _____
11. _____
12. _____
13. _____
14. _____
15. _____
16. _____
17. _____
18. _____
19. _____
20. _____
21. _____
22. _____
23. _____
24. _____
25. _____
26. _____
27. _____
28. _____
29. _____
30. _____
31. _____
32. _____
33. _____
34. _____
35. _____
36. _____
37. _____
38. _____
39. _____
40. _____

Name _____

USING THE ADD MODE

The add mode setting, A, is useful when working with amounts of money. The number of key strokes are reduced because you do not have to press the decimal key with each entry. Rather, each entry is registered as a two-place decimal as soon as you press $+$ or $-$. Cash registers usually use this setting.

You must be careful when entering an amount of money that does not contain a decimal part. This is where the $\boxed{00}$ key comes in handy. With one key stroke, you affix the two zeroes and the number becomes a dollar amount.

DEMONSTRATION EXAMPLE

Set the decimal selector at the add mode.

Add 34.56 + 19.07 + 20

> Press, in order, $\boxed{3}$, $\boxed{4}$, $\boxed{5}$, $\boxed{6}$, $\boxed{+}$
>
> Press $\boxed{1}$, $\boxed{9}$, $\boxed{0}$, $\boxed{7}$, $\boxed{+}$
>
> Press $\boxed{2}$, $\boxed{0}$, $\boxed{00}$, $\boxed{T}$ (or $\boxed{*}$ or $\boxed{+}$)
>
> The answer on the display or tape is 73.63

EXERCISE 2: ADDING DECIMALS

▶ Set the decimal selector at the add mode. Add and write the sums on the answer tab.

1.	7.77	2.	8.88	3.	9.99	4.	1.23	5.	3.33
	7.78		8.89		9.98		3.21		3.32
	7.79		8.87		9.97		2.31		3.11
	7.88		8.77		9.88		3.12		3.22
	7.99		8.99		9.77		1.32		3.21
	<u>7.77</u>		<u>8.88</u>		<u>9.99</u>		<u>2.13</u>		<u>3.33</u>

6.	5.03	7.	9.80	8.	4.00	9.	5.55	10.	7.54
	2.30		8.75		5.12		4.65		8.50
	1.00		1.24		6.35		9.87		5.00
	<u>2.03</u>		<u>7.00</u>		<u>4.50</u>		<u>7.09</u>		<u>6.08</u>

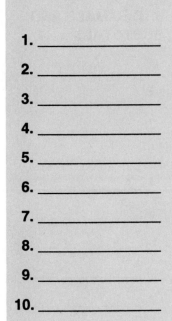

1. _____

2. _____

3. _____

4. _____

5. _____

6. _____

7. _____

8. _____

9. _____

10. _____

Name _____

3. DECIMALS AND SUBTOTALS

1. _____
2. _____
3. _____
4. _____
5. _____
6. _____
   Sub
   _____
   Total
7. _____
   Sub
   _____
   Total
8. _____
   Sub
   _____
   Total
9. _____
   Sub
   _____
   Total
10. _____
    Sub
    _____
    Total
11. _____
    Sub
    _____
    Total
12. _____
    Sub
    _____
    Total
13. _____
    Sub
    _____
    Total
14. _____
    Sub
    _____
    Total
15. _____
    Sub
    _____
    Total

EXERCISE 3: DECIMALS AND SUBTOTALS

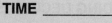 All the numbers in these exercises have two places to the right of the decimal. Use the add mode setting. Remember that with the add mode you do not enter the decimal point. The calculator will include it automatically.

Notice the subtotals in problems 6–15. Use the subtotal key, ⬜S or ◆ . Record the subtotal and then continue the addition or, if you are using a tape, you can read the subtotal from the tape.

1. 4.65	2. 4.44	3. 5.55	4. 6.66	5. 7.89
6.54	4.55	5.44	6.55	9.87
5.46	4.66	5.54	6.44	8.79
6.45	4.45	5.56	6.65	7.98
5.64	4.46	5.66	6.64	8.97
4.56	4.44	5.55	6.66	9.78

6. 2.22	7. 1.11	8. 7.93	9. 8.46	10. 3.49
2.21	1.12	6.84	6.24	8.62
2.23	1.13	1.53	3.65	2.48
Sub	Sub	Sub	Sub	Sub
2.11	1.22	2.46	4.27	5.71
2.33	1.33	7.59	1.83	9.13
2.22	1.11	8.52	9.76	5.60

11. 486.20	12. 895.07	13. 990.03	14. 8,954.10	15. 9.865.32
793.01	230.46	112.00	6,993.03	1,245.78
670.49	451.90	330.70	4,751.10	7,485.96
205.13	673.04	556.00	1,007.72	3,625.41
Sub	Sub	Sub	Sub	Sub
862.80	507.98	881.00	2,335.00	2,356.98
379.01	306.24	220.40	4,480.11	8,754.21
940.76	910.54	445.00	6,017.30	6,958.47
503.12	736.40	770.06	5,664.17	1,452.63

Lesson 3
TOUCH DRILL FOR SPEED DEVELOPMENT

▶ Place your fingers on the home row. Use a printing calculator, adding machine, or 10-key to complete the following problems. All the numbers have two-place decimals, so you may use the add mode. Find each difference and write your answer on the answer tab. Record the total number of minutes and seconds it takes to complete these exercises on the line provided.

1. 5.64 −6.65	2. 8.99 −9.78	3. 1.23 −3.21	4. 7.79 −8.97	5. 2.13 −3.12
6. 7.14 −1.47	7. 5.25 −2.85	8. 9.36 −6.93	9. 8.58 −5.52	10. 7.74 −1.74
11. 6.54 −4.65	12. 5.56 −4.66	13. 2.32 −2.12	14. 3.32 −2.13	15. 9.78 −7.89
16. 9.36 −3.96	17. 8.52 −5.58	18. 7.71 −7.41	19. 7.44 −4.74	20. 3.69 −3.39
21. 6.00 −6.54	22. 8.00 −7.98	23. 3.00 −1.31	24. 9.00 −8.99	25. 3.00 −1.31
26. 7.00 −1.41	27. 6.00 −5.82	28. 9.00 −7.63	29. 5.00 −2.52	30. 7.00 −1.47
31. 6.00 −4.46	32. 5.00 −4.65	33. 4.00 −3.12	34. 3.00 −2.13	35. 9.00 −7.78
36. 9.00 −3.66	37. 8.00 −5.88	38. 7.00 −4.41	39. 7.00 −4.17	40. 9.00 −3.69

▶ Use a standard business calculator to complete the following problems.

41. 9.00 −4.54	42. 7.00 −6.98	43. 8.00 −7.31	44. 9.00 −6.99	45. 7.00 −1.31
46. 4.00 −2.91	47. 8.00 −1.92	48. 7.00 −3.63	49. 6.00 −3.52	50. 8.00 −4.57
51. 8.00 −2.66	52. 6.00 −3.95	53. 5.00 −4.22	54. 5.00 −3.93	55. 7.00 −5.78

Calculating with Decimal Numbers • 37

Lesson 3
APPLY YOUR SKILLS

▶ Many businesses total their sales in inventory using a calculator. The following sales totals show the total receipts for The Sound Shop music store for six consecutive weeks. Total the sales for each week and write your answer on the blank line following the word "Total."

1. Week of _____Feb. 7_____
   Receipts from sale of:
   CDs   307.56
   LPs   119.70
   Tapes   143.65
   Videos   219.96
   Equipment   405.70
   Accessories 94.16
   Sales tax   64.54
   Total   _____

3. Week of _____Feb. 21_____
   Receipts from sale of:
   CDs   585.20
   LPs   186.75
   Tapes   221.90
   Videos   108.63
   Equipment   406.87
   Accessories 176.92
   Sales tax   84.31
   Total   _____

2. Week of _____Feb. 14_____
   Receipts from sale of:
   CDs   395.82
   LPs   126.95
   Tapes   95.40
   Videos   142.73
   Equipment   360.08
   Accessories 129.77
   Sales tax   62.54
   Total   _____

4. Week of _____Feb. 28_____
   Receipts from sale of:
   CDs   621.39
   LPs   274.85
   Tapes   105.46
   Videos   219.25
   Equipment   315.88
   Accessories 186.59
   Sales tax   86.17
   Total   _____

5. Find the total receipts for the four weeks. _____

APPLY YOUR SKILLS (continued)

▶ The Sound Shop must be careful to keep track of its inventory as well as its sales. Inventory is goods that a company purchases and has on hand to sell to customers. The following purchase totals show total items purchased over four consecutive weeks. Total the purchases for each week and write your answer on the blank line after the word "Total." Then total the amount of mechandise purchases and operating expenses and write the sum on the blank line after "Tot expenses."

6. Expenses:
   Week ending ___Nov. 10___
   Merchandise Purchases:
   CDs ___149.67___
   LPs ___78.50___
   Tapes ___43.86___
   Videos ___101.92___
   Equipment ___216.86___
   Accessories ___53.40___
   Total _____
   Operating Expenses:
   Util./Rent ___300.00___
   Supplies ___26.40___
   Maintenance ___52.76___
   Other ___8.19___
   Wages ___425.63___
   Total _____
   Tot expenses _____

7. Expenses:
   Week ending ___Nov. 17___
   Merchandise Purchases:
   CDs ___86.50___
   LPs ___—___
   Tapes ___49.95___
   Videos ___211.81___
   Equipment ___104.95___
   Accessories ___47.63___
   Total _____
   Operating Expenses:
   Util./Rent ___315.95___
   Supplies ___43.68___
   Maintenance ___65.72___
   Other ___29.91___
   Wages ___429.65___
   Total _____
   Tot expenses _____

▶ Find the total expenses for the two weeks for:

8. CDs _____
9. LPs _____
10. Videos _____
11. Tapes _____
12. Util./Rent _____
13. Supplies _____

Name _____

Lesson 3
CHECK YOUR PROGRESS

1. _____

2. _____

3. _____

4. _____

5. _____

6. _____

7. _____

8. _____

9. _____

10. _____

11. _____

12. _____

13. _____

14. _____

▶ Set your decimal selector at 2 and calculate the following. Write your answers on the answer tab.

1. 7.005	2. 9.263	3. 6.02	4. 7.2	5. 4.23
+2.51	−3.89	+8.67	+3.98	−0.78

6. 34.8	7. 80.01	8. 29.95	9. 73.22	10. 68.493
−23.61	−58.00	+45.71	−19.8	+24.38

▶ Use the A mode and calculate the following.

11. 878.48 + 56.01 − 23.61

12. 67.02 − 15.38 + 67.93

13. 70.00 − 36.16 − 48.76

14. Total the following sales:

3.5 in. disks	$	456.92
5 in. disks		617.35
Computer paper		1,793.72
Ribbons		861.04

Lesson 3
MASTERY CHECKPOINT

▶ Set your decimal selector at 2 and calculate the following. Write your answers on the answer tab.

1.	7.453 −6.36	2.	8.78 +8.457	3.	9.9 −8.99	4.	7.36 +5.00	5.	2.015 −0.73
6.	48.98 +89.502	7.	62.60 −32.715	8.	61.8 +90.02	9.	71.00 −29.71	10.	19.64 −11.5

▶ Use the A mode and calculate the following.

11. 78.40 + 34.11 + 90.83

12. 100.09 − 45.98 − 23.78

13. 672.87 − 452.17 + 56.22

14. Total the expenses:

Rent	$ 567.50
Utilities	145.94
Phone	134.72
Mail	67.04

15. How much more was spent on utilities than on phone?

16. What is the total of phone and mail combined?

1. _____
2. _____
3. _____
4. _____
5. _____
6. _____
7. _____
8. _____
9. _____
10. _____
11. _____
12. _____
13. _____
14. _____
15. _____
16. _____

Name _____

PLACE VALUE AND ROUNDING

OBJECTIVES

After completing this lesson you will be able to:

- Determine the place value of a digit in a number.
- Determine the direction of an inequality.
- Round numbers to the required place.

DETERMINING PLACE VALUES

In the number system we use, the digits take on values based on their position in the overall number. The digit 3, for example, may mean thirty or three thousand or three-tenths depending on its placement within a number. Figure 4.1 is a place value chart that shows the value of digits from millions to thousandths.

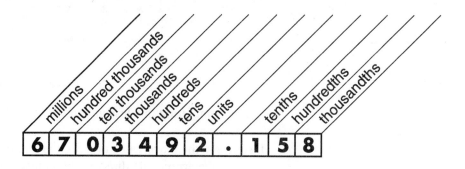

Figure 4.1   Place value chart

DEMONSTRATION EXAMPLE

Determine the place value of the 3 in each of the following numbers:

(a) 1,309.7   (b) 78.035

(a) hundreds   (b) hundredths

EXERCISE 1: PLACE VALUES

▶ Determine the place value of the 5 in each of the following numbers. Write your answers on the answer tab.

1. 65,907.8   2. 673.51   3. 91.025   4. 1,509,781

5. 671.285   6. 5,789,021.7   7. 645   8. 12.75

9. 34,756   10. 457,982   11. 351,902   12. 763.25

▶ Add each of the following. Set your decimal selector so that the answer will be to the nearest hundredth. Write your answers on the answer tab.

13. 36.9 + 15.23 + 79   14. 803 + 76.5 + 32.091

15. 67.44 + 14.92 + 1.1   16. 30 + 67 + 28

1. _____
2. _____
3. _____
4. _____
5. _____
6. _____
7. _____
8. _____
9. _____
10. _____
11. _____
12. _____
13. _____
14. _____
15. _____
16. _____

Name _____

COMPARING NUMBERS

To compare two numbers that are almost the same, read each digit place by place from the left until you come to a digit that is larger in one number than in the other. The number with the larger digit is the larger number. The symbol < means less than. 2 < 3 means "2 is less than 3." The symbol > means greater than. 7 > 2 means "7 is greater than 2." Remember that the large end of "<" opens toward the larger number.

DEMONSTRATION EXAMPLE

Indicate which of the two following numbers is larger. Place < or > on the small blank line between the two numbers.

71.245 __ 71.248   Since 5 < 8, 71.245 < 71.248

EXERCISE 2: GREATER THAN AND LESS THAN

▶ Indicate which number is greater by placing < or > between the numbers.

1. 76 __ 77   2. 4.1 __ 4.2   3. 763.1 __ 763   4. 2.1 __ 2.08

5. 4.551 __ 4.568 6. 234.01 __ 234   7. 8.99 __ 9   8. 6.011 __ 6.002

9. 8.7 __ 8   10. 1,234 __ 234   11. 13.07 __ 14   12. 0.099 __ 0.1

▶ Add or subtract as indicated to find the values of A and B. Write your answers on the blank lines following A and B. Then complete the inequality for A and B by inserting < or > on the blank line between the two letters. Set the decimal selector at 2.

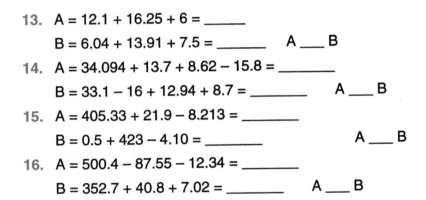

13. A = 12.1 + 16.25 + 6 = _____
     B = 6.04 + 13.91 + 7.5 = _____   A ___ B
14. A = 34.094 + 13.7 + 8.62 – 15.8 = _____
     B = 33.1 – 16 + 12.94 + 8.7 = _____   A ___ B
15. A = 405.33 + 21.9 – 8.213 = _____
     B = 0.5 + 423 – 4.10 = _____   A ___ B
16. A = 500.4 – 87.55 – 12.34 = _____
     B = 352.7 + 40.8 + 7.02 = _____   A ___ B

Name _____

ROUNDING

Sometimes exact numbers are not needed. For example, the manager of a large department may want to know monthly sales or expenses to the nearest hundred dollars. A newspaper might publish figures to the nearest thousand. So it is important for you to know how to round numbers.

To round a number, draw a line under the digit in the rounding place—that is, the place to which you are rounding. This may be tens or hundreds or thousands. Then look at the digit to the right of the rounding place. If that digit is 5 or greater, increase the digit in the rounding place by one and affix zeroes to the right of the rounding place to make the number the required size. If the digit to the right of the rounding place is less than 5, leave the digit in the rounding place unchanged and affix zeroes to the right of that number.

If the rounding place is in the decimal part of a number, follow the same procedure. But in a decimal, you drop any zeroes that appear to the right of the rounded digit.

DEMONSTRATION EXAMPLE

Round each of the following:

(a)   4,651 to the nearest hundred

4,651; 5 is 5 or greater. Increase the 6. The number is rounded to 4,700

(b)   67.034 to the nearest hundredth

67.034; 4 is less than 5. Leave the 3. The number rounded is 67.03

EXERCISE 3: ROUNDING NUMBERS

▶ Round each number to the nearest thousand. Write your answers on the answer tab.

1. 345,671   2. 8,945,501   3. 76,099   4. 2,900

▶ Round each number to the nearest tenth. Write your answers on the answer tab.

5. 34.841   6. 1.025   7. 3.499   8. 675.901

▶ Round each number to the nearest hundredth. Write your answers on the answer tab.

9. 6.785   10. 40.005   11. 3.991   12. 0.088

▶ Round to the nearest unit. Write your answers on the answer tab.

13. 678.53   14. 1,267.49   15. 39.95   16. 5.07

▶ Round to the nearest dollar. Write your answers on the answer tab.

17. $45.75   18. $7.01   19. $9.50   20. $0.60

1. _____
2. _____
3. _____
4. _____
5. _____
6. _____
7. _____
8. _____
9. _____
10. _____
11. _____
12. _____
13. _____
14. _____
15. _____
16. _____
17. _____
18. _____
19. _____
20. _____

Name _____

1. _____

2. _____

3. _____

4. _____

5. _____

6. _____

7. _____

8. _____

9. _____

10. _____

11. _____

12. _____

13. _____

14. _____

15. _____

16. _____

17. _____

18. _____

19. _____

20. _____

21. _____

22. _____

23. _____

24. _____

Lesson 4
TOUCH DRILL FOR SPEED DEVELOPMENT

▶ Add the following sets of numbers. Set your decimal indicator at 0. Write your answers on the answer tab. Record the total number of minutes and seconds it takes to complete these exercises on the line provided.

1.	26,539	2.	57,210	3.	10,026	4.	76,205
	3,498		801		76,251		78
	45,871		6,049		97		8,076
	670		34,073		8,902		67,903
	5,081		46		87,008		676

5.	890,782	6.	102,043	7.	783,501	8.	501,219
	76,233		9,012		820,026		99,201
	5,760		450,023		67,445		78,909
	561		67,905		3,090		601,452
	4,091		3,491		100,672		7,561

▶ Set your decimal indicator at A.

9.	877.01	10.	531.98	11.	764.50	12.	307.12
	86.51		80.95		6.74		148.09
	223.13		8.98		456.56		87.97
	47.17		98.58		79.02		7.11

13.	967.02	14.	76.50	15.	687.45	16.	780.03
	50.01		79.59		98.00		671.83
	78.02		6.41		980.76		78.45

▶ Subtract. Leave your decimal indicator set at A.

17.	45.90	18.	79.04	19.	10.63	20.	78.00
	−17.65		−64.07		−10.09		− 4.98

21.	87.67	22.	87.99	23.	79.87	24.	61.00
	−32.45		− 9.08		− 8.32		− 9.08

Lesson 4
APPLY YOUR SKILLS

When using a calculator, it is important to do quick mental estimates. Then, if you make a keying mistake, you will notice that the answer is not reasonable. Rounding often helps in estimating. Using the touch system to multiply will be taught in the next lesson. You may look at the keys if necessary for this exercise in estimating.

DEMONSTRATION EXAMPLE

Estimate 20 x $1.95

Round 1.95 to 2. 20 x 2 = 40. $40 is a good estimate.

▶ Estimate each of the following to the nearest dollar. Write your estimate in the Estimate column. Then find the actual answer and write your answer in the Actual column.

Food Shipment	Estimate	Actual
5 boxes of cereal at $2.89 a box	1. _____	2. _____
8 pounds of carrots at $0.49 a pound	3. _____	4. _____
12 gallons of milk at $2.56 gallon	5. _____	6. _____
10 quarts of juice at $1.65 a quart	7. _____	8. _____
20 cans of soup at $0.95 a can	9. _____	10. _____

Office Supplies Shipment	Estimate	Actual
25 disks at $3.90 a disk	11. _____	12. _____
15 ribbons at $6.75 each	13. _____	14. _____
30 calculators at $9.65 each	15. _____	16. _____
50 notebooks at $0.99 each	17. _____	18. _____
18 boxes of folders at $19.95 a box	19. _____	20. _____

Office Furniture Shipment	Estimate	Actual
3 chairs at $79.50 each	21. _____	22. _____
6 file cabinets at $89.00 each	23. _____	24. _____
12 computer tables at $119.50 each	25. _____	26. _____
2 bookcases at $189.76 each	27. _____	28. _____
5 tables at $104.60 each	29. _____	30. _____

Name _____

CHECK YOUR PROGRESS sidebar

1. _____

2. _____

3. _____

4. _____

5. _____

6. _____

7. _____

8. _____

9. _____

10. _____

11. _____

12. _____

13. _____
   Exact Answer

   _____
   Rounded Answer

14. _____
   Exact Answer

   _____
   Rounded Answer

15. _____
   Exact Answer

   _____
   Rounded Answer

Lesson 4
CHECK YOUR PROGRESS

▶ Determine the place value of the 6 in each of the following numbers. Write your answers on the answer tab.

1. 8,679,043   2. 97.061   3. 76.4   4. 2.006

_____   _____   _____   _____

▶ Indicate which of the following pairs of numbers is greater by placing < or > between the numbers.

5. 23.01 ___ 23.1   6. 67.11 ___ 67.05   7. 43.99 ___ 44   8. 6.89 ___ 6.891

▶ Round each of the following numbers to the nearest tenth.

9. 56.56   10. 4.99   11. 78.055   12. 54.012

_____   _____   _____   _____

▶ Calculate the exact answer then round each answer to the nearest whole number.

		Exact Answer	Rounded Answer
13.	$9.82 + 9.77 + 103.2$	_____	_____
14.	$19.3 - 0.5 + 11.2 - 19.8$	_____	_____
15.	$7.3 + 2.9 - 3.9$	_____	_____

Name _____   52 • Lesson 4

Lesson 4
MASTERY CHECKPOINT

▶ Determine the place value of the 4 in each of the following numbers.

1. 679,043   2. 2,097.46   3. 764,905   4. 3.054

_____   _____   _____   _____

▶ Indicate which number is greater by placing < or > between the following pairs of numbers.

5. 3.01 __ 3.1   6. 6.15 __ 6.152   7. 3.99 __ 4.01   8. 2.08 __ 2.11

▶ Round each number to the nearest unit.

9. 23.45   10. 617.89   11. 9.99   12. 3,854.09

_____   _____   _____   _____

▶ Estimate each answer to the nearest whole number. Then calculate the exact answer.

		Estimate	Exact Answer
13.	$11.82 + 9.77 - 20.1$	_____	_____
14.	$9.3 + 11.2 - 101.3$	_____	_____
15.	$17.3 + 2.9 - 6.5 + 3.5$	_____	_____

1. _____

2. _____

3. _____

4. _____

5. _____

6. _____

7. _____

8. _____

9. _____

10. _____

11. _____

12. _____

13. _____
      Estimate

_____
     Exact Answer

14. _____
      Estimate

_____
     Exact Answer

15. _____
      Estimate

_____
     Exact Answer

Name _____

MULTIPLICATION OF WHOLE NUMBERS AND DECIMALS

OBJECTIVES

After completing this lesson you will be able to:

- Use the touch system to multiply whole numbers and decimals;
- Solve business math problems requiring multiplication.

USING THE TOUCH SYSTEM TO MULTIPLY

Multiplication is repeated addition. Thus, 4 x 3 means 3 added to itself 4 times. The two numbers multiplied are called factors. The result is the product. Knowing the basic multiplication facts will help you see whether an answer is approximately right. When multiplying decimal numbers, the calculator will take care of the placement of the decimal point in the answer. But, again, you should be sure that you spot any mistake you may make in using the calculator. Remember to set the decimal selector to the number of places desired in your answer. In general, you will want as many decimal places in the product (answer) as there are in the two factors combined.

To find the answer when multiplying or dividing, press the $=$ key, not T or $*$ as when adding or subtracting.

DEMONSTRATION EXAMPLE 1

Multiply 37 x 4.95. Check that your answer is reasonable.

      Rounding and doing mental math: 40 x 5 = 200

      Enter the keys in the order shown: 37 x 4.95 = 183.15

      The answer is 183.15. This close to 200.

EXERCISE 1: MULTIPLYING WHOLE NUMBERS

▶ Multiply each of the following. Remember to return your fingers to the home row after each entry. Write your answers on the answer tab.

1.	23 x 47	2.	82 x 54
3.	64 x 98	4.	90 x 20
5.	25 x 64	6.	18 x 81
7.	67 x 78	8.	60 x 44
9.	41 x 41	10.	78 x 52
11.	9 x 231	12.	8 x 476
13.	7 x 109	14.	6 x 830
15.	5 x 200	16.	4 x 351
17.	3 x 827	18.	2 x 874
19.	42 x 301	20.	71 x 496

1. _____
2. _____
3. _____
4. _____
5. _____
6. _____
7. _____
8. _____
9. _____
10. _____
11. _____
12. _____
13. _____
14. _____
15. _____
16. _____
17. _____
18. _____
19. _____
20. _____

Name _____

1. _____
2. _____
3. _____
4. _____
5. _____
6. _____
7. _____
8. _____
9. _____
10. _____
11. _____
12. _____
13. _____
14. _____
15. _____
16. _____
17. _____
18. _____
19. _____
20. _____
21. _____
22. _____
23. _____
24. _____
25. _____
26. _____
27. _____
28. _____
29. _____
30. _____
31. _____
32. _____
33. _____
34. _____
35. _____
36. _____

EXERCISE 2: MULTIPLYING DECIMAL NUMBERS

▶ Multiply each of the following. It is common to place a 0 before the decimal point when writing a decimal number less than 1. For example, 0.8. The 0 draws attention to the decimal point, which might otherwise be overlooked. When entering such a number in your calculator, it is not necessary to enter the 0. But the 0 will appear in the display.

For the following exercises, set your decimal selector at 2. Write your answers on the answer tab.

1.	0.2 x 45	2.	0.9 x 64
3.	0.5 x 89	4.	0.3 x 72
5.	0.8 x 30	6.	0.7 x 37
7.	0.1 x 49	8.	0.4 x 99
9.	0.6 x 0.5	10.	0.6 x 0.6
11.	0.4 x 0.9	12.	0.7 x 0.9
13.	4.5 x 76	14.	6.8 x 47
15.	8.2 x 65	16.	9.9 x 40
17.	2.5 x 5.8	18.	9.4 x 2.7
19.	6.7 x 9.2	20.	6.6 x 7.7
21.	5 x 5.67	22.	6 x 9.82
23.	9 x 4.61	24.	7 x 9.02
25.	4.5 x 89.1	26.	9.6 x 87.5
27.	1.7 x 98.4	28.	8.3 x 6.22
29.	35 x 5.89	30.	55 x 2.98
31.	74 x 9.25	32.	60 x 9.95
33.	18 x 3.10	34.	74 x 3.50
35.	26 x 8.87	36.	44 x 2.98

Name _____

EXERCISE 3: MULTIPLYING INTERMEDIATE PRODUCTS

▶ In all these problems, you will need to multiply intermediate products by new multiplers. Be sure to record each intermediate product *before* you go on with the problem. If you are using a display calculator, you will not be able to go back later and find the intermediate products. Set the decimal selector at 4.

	Factor	x	Factor	=	Product	x	Factor	=	Product	x	Factor	=	Product
1.	28.0842	x	35.141	=	_____	x	1.0923	=	_____	x	.5672	=	_____
2.	12.87	x	.0062	=	_____	x	8.6324	=	_____	x	1.0691	=	_____
3.	.09	x	1.389	=	_____	x	67.89	=	_____	x	2.34252	=	_____
4.	31.141	x	9.8734	=	_____	x	8.5189	=	_____	x	.3406	=	_____
5.	268.04	x	3.176	=	_____	x	35.491	=	_____	x	.8015	=	_____
6.	79.033	x	2.081	=	_____	x	10.073	=	_____	x	42.905	=	_____
7.	.00678	x	8.93217	=	_____	x	42.6	=	_____	x	8.9031	=	_____
8.	87.5431	x	9.2865	=	_____	x	1.4327	=	_____	x	2.9029	=	_____
9.	3.598	x	.076324	=	_____	x	.81974	=	_____	x	13.49	=	_____
10.	.153	x	.08752	=	_____	x	.0425	=	_____	x	.987	=	_____
11.	26.90354	x	.46781	=	_____	x	.03548	=	_____	x	682.1	=	_____
12.	1,012.67	x	.87632	=	_____	x	.49835	=	_____	x	.09267	=	_____
13.	.13465	x	.7928	=	_____	x	.4056	=	_____	x	5.414	=	_____
14.	.4785	x	1.6727	=	_____	x	67.151	=	_____	x	60.43	=	_____
15.	.5987	x	.1654	=	_____	x	3.912	=	_____	x	6.84357	=	_____
16.	46.6	x	92.79	=	_____	x	18.507	=	_____	x	.923	=	_____

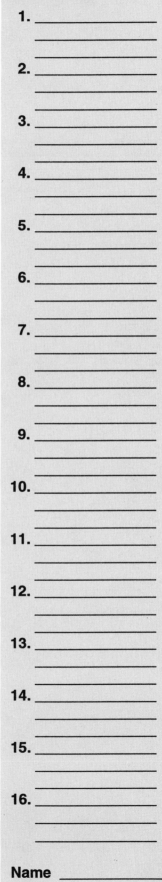

3. MULTIPLYING INTERMEDIATE PRODUCTS

1. _____

2. _____

3. _____

4. _____

5. _____

6. _____

7. _____

8. _____

9. _____

10. _____

11. _____

12. _____

13. _____

14. _____

15. _____

16. _____

Name _____

INVOICES

An invoice is a bill sent by a company or individual. It shows products or services purchased and the amount of payment required. For each item there is listed a quantity, a unit price, and a total. The total amount for that item is found by multiplying the unit price by the quantity.

EXERCISE 4: TOTALING INVOICES

▶ Find the total amount for each item below and then find the total for all the items on the invoice.

Quantity	Item	Unit Price	Amount
24	CDs	$ 8.45	1. _____
58	Blank video tapes	1.95	2. _____
172	LPs	4.50	3. _____
55	Videos	9.90	4. _____
		Total	5. _____

Quantity	Item	Unit Price	Amount
23 doz	Disks	$ 23.85 a doz	6. _____
60 cartons	Computer paper	29.50 a carton	7. _____
54 boxes	Ribbons	46.75 a box	8. _____
19	Calculators	17.95 ea	9. _____
		Total	10. _____

Quantity	Item	Unit Price	Amount
15 cartons	Cereal	$22.65 a carton	11. _____
60	Bread	0.89 a loaf	12. _____
30 doz	Rolls	2.75 a doz	13. _____
64	Cakes	3.45 ea	14. _____
		Total	15. _____

Quantity	Item	Unit Price	Amount
14 boxes	Folders	$14.95 a box	16. _____
55 boxes	Pens	1.80 a box	17. _____
30 doz	Notebooks	19.50 a doz	18. _____
44 doz	Rulers	4.76 a doz	19. _____
		Total	20. _____

Name _____

Lesson 5
APPLY YOUR SKILLS

▶ For the following invoices, find the amounts, the subtotals, and the totals.

CANAAN TIRE AND AUTO REPAIR

Quantity	Item	Unit Price	Amount
4	Tires	$ 28.45	1. _____
6	Spark plugs	2.39	2. _____
2	Shock absorbers	19.95	3. _____
		Subtotal, parts	4. _____
18 hrs	Labor	$ 24.50 per hr	5. _____
		Total	6. _____

MIDTOWN COMPUTER CENTER

Quantity	Item	Unit Price	Amount
9 boxes	Disks	$ 19.70 a box	7. _____
15 boxes	Ribbons	34.80 a box	8. _____
1	Memory board	127.95 ea	9. _____
		Subtotal, materials	10. _____
7.5 hours	Labor	$ 19.60 per hr	11. _____
		Total	12. _____

ELECTRONIC WORLD

Quantity	Item	Unit Price	Amount
5	CDs	$ 12.95 ea	13. _____
20	Tapes	3.89 ea	14. _____
3	Fuses	3.75 ea	15. _____
		Subtotal, materials	16. _____
5.5 hrs	Labor	$ 18.40 per hr	17. _____
		Total	18. _____

CHECK YOUR PROGRESS

▶ Perform the indicated operations. Set your decimal selector at 2. Write your answers on the answer tab.

1.	25 x 67	2.	32 x 94
3.	24 x 18	4.	80 x 93
5.	2.7 x 60	6.	61 x 7.1
7.	6.3 x 28	8.	6.6 x 50
9.	3.2 x 6.1	10.	4.8 x 9.2

11. 6.40	12. 5.87	13. 4.80	14. 8.65	15. 7.68
−9.65	−4.27	−2.12	−3.71	−2.67

16. 9.30	17. 5.89	18. 2.81	19. 5.04	20. 8.89
−2.06	−1.09	−1.99	−4.70	−3.49

▶ Find the total amounts for the following invoice.

Quantity	Item	Unit Price		Amount
35 pair	Athletic shoes	$ 44.95 ea	21.	
16 doz	T-shirts	21.80 a doz	22.	
30	Tennis rackets	49.50 ea	23.	
		Total	24.	

1. _____
2. _____
3. _____
4. _____
5. _____
6. _____
7. _____
8. _____
9. _____
10. _____
11. _____
12. _____
13. _____
14. _____
15. _____
16. _____
17. _____
18. _____
19. _____
20. _____
21. _____
22. _____
23. _____
24. _____

Name _____

Lesson 5
MASTERY CHECKPOINT

▶ Perform the indicated operations. For 1–6, set your decimal selector at 2.

1. 7.8 x 5.2
2. 92 x 0.64
3. 6.4 x 2.8
4. 0.7 x 0.31
5. 6.7 x 70
6. 81 x 9.3

▶ Find the total amounts for the following invoice.

Quantity	Item	Unit Price	Amount
76 pr	Sox	$ 2.95 ea	7. _____
20 doz	Shorts	24.55 a doz	8. _____
45 pr	Skis	119.50 a pr	9. _____
		Total	10. _____

LESSON **6**

DIVISION OF WHOLE NUMBERS AND DECIMALS

OBJECTIVES

After completing this lesson, you will be able to:

- Use the touch system to divide whole numbers and decimals.
- Convert fractions and mixed numbers to decimals.
- Solve business math problems requiring division.

USING DIVISION

In division, you separate a number of objects or an amount of money into a number of equal parts. You use division to calculate averages, rates (such as miles per hour), and unit costs (such as cost per ounce). Division is also used to convert fractions and mixed numbers to decimal numbers. A mixed number, such as 2 3/4, combines a whole number and a fraction. In an improper fraction, such as 5/2, the top number is larger than the bottom number. Since calculators and computers are so widely used, decimal numbers are used more frequently than fractions. Remember, you must use the $=$ key for the answer.

DEMONSTRATION EXAMPLE

Divide $456.70 by 28. Set the decimal selector at 2.

Enter the amount of money, then the function and the divisor. Then press the $=$ key.

$456.7 \div 28 = 16.31$

In the example, 456.70 is the dividend, 28 is the divisor, and 16.31 is the quotient.

EXERCISE 1: DIVIDING DECIMALS

▶ Divide to find each answer. Remember to continue using the touch method. Set your decimal selector at 2.

1.	420.5 ÷ 9	2.	507.2 ÷ 7
3.	902.7 ÷ 5	4.	676.9 ÷ 8
5.	324.12 ÷ 15	6.	879.17 ÷ 17
7.	606.08 ÷ 22	8.	987.34 ÷ 13
9.	5,050.42 ÷ 6	10.	7,512.30 ÷ 25
11.	7,002.15 ÷ 54	12.	9,005.63 ÷ 34
13.	789 ÷ 2.5	14.	603 ÷ 5.6
15.	450 ÷ 1.8	16.	211 ÷ 8.7
17.	470 ÷ 4.5	18.	670 ÷ 3.6
19.	6.5 ÷ 2.1	20.	8.9 ÷ 4.5
21.	19.5 ÷ 0.5	22.	43.8 ÷ 0.6
23.	34.9 ÷ 0.9	24.	3.4 ÷ 6.5
25.	906 ÷ 21	26.	831 ÷ 14
27.	7,030 ÷ 312	28.	6,782 ÷ 32
29.	8,700 ÷ 2.15	30.	7,061 ÷ 7.5

1. _____
2. _____
3. _____
4. _____
5. _____
6. _____
7. _____
8. _____
9. _____
10. _____
11. _____
12. _____
13. _____
14. _____
15. _____
16. _____
17. _____
18. _____
19. _____
20. _____
21. _____
22. _____
23. _____
24. _____
25. _____
26. _____
27. _____
28. _____
29. _____
30. _____

Name _____

FRACTIONS AND DECIMALS

A fraction indicates part of a whole. For example, one-fifth (1/5) means one part out of five. A fraction also shows one number divided by another. To convert a fraction to a decimal, you simply divide the numerator (top number) by the denominator (bottom number).

$$\frac{3}{4} \qquad \begin{array}{l}\text{numerator} \\ \text{denominator}\end{array} \qquad 3 \div 4 = 0.75$$

DEMONSTRATION EXAMPLE

Convert the following fractions to decimals. Then arrange the numbers in order from least to greatest. Round each decimal to two places by setting your decimal selector at 2.

1/2, 3/10, 9/7

Using a calculator to divide each numerator by each denominator:

$1 \div 2 = 0.50$

$3 \div 10 = 0.30$

$9 \div 7 = 1.29$

The order is the same as it would be for whole numbers:

0.30, 0.50, 1.29

EXERCISE 2: CONVERTING FRACTIONS TO DECIMALS

▶ In the following sets of fractions, convert each fraction to a decimal. Then arrange the decimals in order from least to greatest.

1. 2/3 = _____, 3/4 = _____, 5/8 = _____, 4/10 = _____

   Correct order _____

2. 6/7 = _____, 7/8 = _____, 4/5 = _____, 1/4 = _____

   Correct order _____

3. 5/9 = _____, 7/25 = _____, 6/15 = _____, 9/20 = _____

   Correct order _____

4. 37/50 = _____, 7/11 = _____, 8/16 = _____, 8/19 =_____

   Correct order _____

▶ Convert the following improper fractions to decimal numbers. Then arrange your answers in order from least to greatest.

5. 9/6 = _____, 20/17 = _____, 10/7 = _____, 15/9 = _____

   Correct order _____

6. 25/8 = _____, 30/13 = _____, 21/10 = _____, 18/11 = _____

   Correct order _____

7. 30/12 = _____, 36/18 = _____, 50/21 = _____, 25/9 = _____

   Correct order _____

8. 35/10 = _____, 52/17 = _____, 98/39 = _____, 65/31 = _____

   Correct order _____

Name _____

EXERCISE 3: FRACTION/DECIMAL CONVERSION

▶ Remember that to convert a fraction to a decimal, you divide the numerator by the denominator. Convert the following fractions to decimals, and study the answers as you do. It will be helpful in your business work if you know some of the basic fraction/ decimal conversions.

1. 1/2 =_____   2. 1/3 =_____   3. 2/3 = _____

4. 1/4 =_____   5. 2/4 =_____   6. 3/4 = _____

7. 1/5 =_____   8. 2/5 =_____   9. 3/5 = _____

10. 4/5 =_____   11. 1/6 =_____   12. 2/6 = _____

13. 3/6 =_____   14. 4/6 =_____   15. 5/6 = _____

16. 1/7 =_____   17. 2/7 =_____   18. 3/7 = _____

19. 4/7 =_____   20. 5/7 =_____   21. 6/7 = _____

22. 1/8 =_____   23. 2/8 =_____   24. 3/8 = _____

25. 4/8 =_____   26. 5/8 =_____   27. 6/8 = _____

28. 7/8 =_____   29. 1/9 =_____   30. 2/9 = _____

31. 3/9 =_____   32. 4/9 =_____   33. 5/9 = _____

34. 6/9 =_____   35. 7/9 =_____   36. 8/9 = _____

37. 1/10 =_____   38. 2/10 =_____   39. 5/10 = _____

40. 7/10 =_____   41. 3/20 =_____   42. 5/20 = _____

43. 7/20 =_____   44. 9/20 =_____   45. 10/20 = _____

46. 11/20 =_____ 47. 17/20 =_____ 48. 19/20 = _____

49. 1/25 =_____   50. 6/25 =_____   51. 7/25 = _____

52. 11/25 =_____ 53. 15/25 =_____ 54. 21/25 = _____

55. 1/40 =_____   56. 21/40 =_____ 57. 3/50 = _____

58. 9/50 =_____   59. 17/100 =_____ 60. 19/100 = _____

EXERCISE 4: CONVERTING TIME

▶ Time is often converted from hours and minutes to decimal.

DEMONSTRATION EXAMPLE

Convert 4 hours and 35 minutes to a decimal form of hours.

There are 60 minutes in an hour. 35/60 = 0.58

4 hr 35 min = 4.58 hr

▶ Convert each of the following to a decimal form of hours. Set your calculator for 2 decimal places.

1. 3 hr 15 min = _____

2. 7 hr 20 min = _____

3. 6 hr 30 min = _____

4. 8 hr 10 min = _____

5. 5 hr 14 min = _____

6. 2 hr 5 min = _____

7. 4 hr 50 min = _____

8. 1 hr 45 min = _____

9. 2 hr 40 min = _____

10. 6 hr 18 min = _____

Name _____

EXERCISE 5: DETERMINING MILES PER HOUR

▶ Miles per hour is the average speed or rate. It is found by dividing total miles driven by total time. If you drive 200 miles in 5 hours, then your average rate of speed is 200 ÷ 5 = 40 miles per hour.

The following table shows miles driven and time for different drivers. Complete the table by finding totals and miles per hour for each driver.

Driver		Mon.	Tues.	Wed.	Thurs.	Fri.	Total	Miles per hr.
1.	Miles	245	354	401	278	350	_____	
	Hours	4.7	6.8	7.5	5.6	6.4	_____	_____
2.	Miles	501	467	386	529	461	_____	
	Hours	11.1	7.4	6.9	9.3	7.7	_____	_____
3.	Miles	352	299	521	234	315	_____	
	Hours	5.8	5.2	9.7	4.6	5.6	_____	_____
4.	Miles	187	203	165	245	143	_____	
	Hours	6.4	5.5	4.3	6.1	4.2	_____	_____
5.	Miles	99	124	203	145	178	_____	
	Hours	3.8	4.3	4.9	4.4	4.5	_____	_____

Lesson 6
APPLY YOUR SKILLS

Many people drive as part of their work. For long-distance truck drivers and delivery drivers, driving is almost all of their work. Others, such as salespersons, sometimes drive as part of their work. In both cases, records of gas usage and miles covered are important.

DEMONSTRATION EXAMPLE

The table below shows miles driven and gas purchased during one week. Find total miles, gas purchased, and average miles per gallon.

	Mon.	Tues.	Wed.	Thurs.	Fri.	Total
Miles	462	301	345	260	187	<u>1555</u>
Gallons	28.5	15.3	18.7	14.9	11.2	<u>88.6</u>

To find total miles and total gallons, you add the daily amounts.

To find the average miles per gallon, you divide miles by gallons.

$1555 \div 88.6 = 17.55$ average miles per gallon

▶ Five company drivers turned in the weekly miles driven and gallons of gas purchased as shown below. For each of these, find the total miles driven, the total gallons purchased, and the average miles per gallon.

1.

	Mon.	Tues.	Wed.	Thurs.	Fri.	Total
Miles	119	245	267	107	321	_____
Gallons	5.4	11.5	13.5	6.3	15.8	_____

Average miles per gallon _____

2.

	Mon.	Tues.	Wed.	Thurs.	Fri.	Total
Miles	304	517	236	435	288	_____
Gallons	25.3	41.7	18.4	35.1	22.6	_____

Average miles per gallon _____

3.

	Mon.	Tues.	Wed.	Thurs.	Fri.	Total
Miles	435	401	476	423	418	_____
Gallons	28	25.3	30.3	16.9	25.4	_____

Average miles per gallon _____

4.

	Mon.	Tues.	Wed.	Thurs.	Fri.	Total
Miles	256	341	546	93	380	_____
Gallons	28.4	36.5	60.2	7.3	39.7	_____

Average miles per gallon _____

Name _____

Lesson 6
CHECK YOUR PROGRESS

▶ Divide to find each answer. Remember to continue using the touch method. Set your decimal selector at 2.

1. $345.9 \div 8$ = _____
2. $905.3 \div 6$ = _____
3. $875.3 \div 9$ = _____
4. $310.23 \div 4$ = _____
5. $762.12 \div 13$ = _____
6. $564.17 \div 25$ = _____
7. $679.08 \div 24$ = _____
8. $826.05 \div 19$ = _____
9. $5,987.42 \div 7$ = _____
10. $7,894.90 \div 28$ = _____

▶ In the following sets of fractions, convert each fraction to a decimal. Then arrange the decimals in order from least to greatest. Set the decimal selector at 2.

11. 2/5 = _____, 3/4 = _____, 5/9 = _____, 4/7 = _____

    Correct order: _____

12. 6/10 = _____, 5/8 = _____, 4/9 = _____, 5/6 = _____

    Correct order: _____

Lesson 6
MASTERY CHECKPOINT

▶ Divide to find each answer. Remember to continue using the touch method.
Set your decimal selector at 2.

1. 5,469.08 ÷ 21 = _____

2. 9,705.32 ÷ 16 = _____

3. 8,477.03 ÷ 19 = _____

4. 3,780.03 ÷ 14 = _____

5. 1,792.12 ÷ 23 = _____

6. 5,104.27 ÷ 15 = _____

7. 6,509.08 ÷ 13 = _____

8. 2,806.05 ÷ 29 = _____

9. 6,917.42 ÷ 17 = _____

10. 3,094.98 ÷ 18 = _____

▶ Calculate the total miles and average miles per week.

Driver	Week 1	2	3	4	5	Total	Average Miles per Week
A	346.63	413.44	782.97	393.87	498.99		
B	547.58	498.27	516.28	395.55	397.74		
C	405.76	509.12	393.81	417.59	391.75		
D	572.09	390.75	481.83	515.08	501.82		
E	474.77	401.68	393.38	496.39	422.87		
F	372.35	438.91	315.95	457.83	361.00		

Name _____

USE OF THE CONSTANT

OBJECTIVES

After completing this lesson, you will be able to:

- Use the constant function in multiplication and division.
- Solve business problems involving the use of a constant.

USING THE CONSTANT IN MULTIPLICATION

On most business calculators you can save time when multiplying several numbers by the same number. The number that is repeated is called a constant and once entered can be used over and over without being rekeyed. For example, if you are calculating earnings and the hourly rate is the same for all employees, you must multiply many different numbers of hours by $7.36 (the hourly rate). The hourly rate is the constant and has to be entered only once.

Your calculator might automatically hold the first number entered or there might be a constant setting, $\boxed{\text{K}}$, to be used. In either case, entering the constant first and then pressing $\boxed{\text{x}}$ followed by the other factor and $\boxed{=}$ will give the answer. It is only necessary to press the multiplication key, $\boxed{\text{x}}$, for the first problem. After that, entering the second number and $\boxed{=}$ will give the answer. Check the manual for your calculator and talk with your teacher about the use of the constant.

DEMONSTRATION EXAMPLE

Use a constant multiplier to find the following wages. The workers each earn $7.36 per hour. To find their wages, multiply the rate per hour by the number of hours worked.

Able	7.36 x 9
Bernstein	7.36 x 25
Cortez	7.36 x 38.5
Dissell	7.36 x 17.5

If you have a constant switch, set it to K. Set the decimal selector at 2.

Enter		Display
7.36 x 9	=	66.24
25	=	184.00
38.5	=	283.36
17.5	=	128.80

EXERCISE 1: USING THE CONSTANT FUNCTION TO MULTIPLY

▶ Use the constant function to find the products. Remember that the constant number must be entered first. Use the floating decimal setting. Round each answer to the greatest number of places found in any one factor. For example, round the answer of 3.45 x 1.087 to three places. Write your answers on the tab provided.

1.	364	x	35
	298	x	35
	67	x	35
	209	x	35

2.	29.67	x	13.1
	108.52	x	13.1
	96.03	x	13.1
	6.009	x	13.1

3.	5.006	x	6.71
	26.01	x	6.71
	11.35	x	6.71
	49.8	x	6.71

4.	12.1	x	.098
	14.9	x	.098
	17.6	x	.098
	15.8	x	.098

5.	1.006	x	4.01
	.493	x	4.01
	23.1	x	4.01
	8.67	x	4.01

6.	3.142	x	5.013
	.987	x	5.013
	21.34	x	5.013
	66.123	x	5.013

7.	123.4	x	13.42
	69.8	x	13.42
	119.6	x	13.42
	46.5	x	13.42

8.	68.78	x	1.009
	9.53	x	1.009
	35.9	x	1.009
	7.1	x	1.009

9.	.453	x	.097
	.453	x	.689
	.453	x	.992
	.453	x	.886

10.	16.89	x	134
	16.89	x	12.892
	16.89	x	9.775
	16.89	x	.832

11.	6.25	x	28
	6.25	x	316
	6.25	x	904
	6.25	x	37

12.	1.08	x	10
	1.08	x	16.6
	1.08	x	359
	1.08	x	705

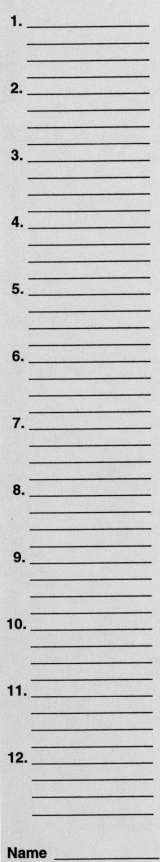

1. USING THE CONSTANT FUNCTION TO MULTIPLY

1. _____
_____
_____
_____

2. _____
_____
_____
_____

3. _____
_____
_____

4. _____
_____
_____
_____

5. _____
_____
_____

6. _____
_____
_____
_____

7. _____
_____
_____
_____

8. _____
_____
_____

9. _____
_____
_____
_____

10. _____
_____
_____

11. _____
_____
_____
_____

12. _____
_____
_____
_____

Name _____

USING THE CONSTANT IN DIVISION

The constant can be used for division as well as multiplication.

DEMONSTRATION EXAMPLE

Use the constant for the following:

$$78.45 \div 7.5$$

$$21.09 \div 7.5$$

$$18.00 \div 7.5$$

Set the decimal selector at 2. Set the constant function on K. In this case, the divisor is the constant and should be entered after the dividend and the division symbol. For the second and third problems, you enter only the dividend and press ☐ =.

Enter		Display
78.45 ÷ 7.5	=	10.46
21.09	=	2.81
18	=	2.40

EXERCISE 2: USING THE CONSTANT FUNCTION TO DIVIDE

▶ The XRL Company is changing the pay scale for some of its employees, from a weekly amount to an hourly rate. Use the constant function to divide each weekly amount by 40 (the number of hours worked per week) and compute the hourly rate. Set the decimal selector at 2.

Weekly Amount	Hourly Rate	Weekly Amount	Hourly Rate
1. $240	_____	2. $287	_____
3. $316	_____	4. $320.40	_____
5. $352.50	_____	6. $389.25	_____
7. $420	_____	8. $473.28	_____
9. $502.06	_____	10. $595.77	_____

▶ The following employees are paid biweekly (once every two weeks). Divide their salaries by 80 (the number of hours worked in two weeks) to establish an hourly rate.

11. $1,100	_____	12. $1,246.70	_____
13. $1,258.74	_____	14. $1,297.29	_____
15. $1,350.60	_____	16. $1,420.00	_____
17. $1,500.50	_____	18. $1,515.25	_____
19. $1,600	_____	20. $1,620.80	_____

Name _____

AVERAGES

Division is used to find averages. You have seen how a company that is responsible for deliveries might want to know about average miles per gallon and average miles per hour. Such a company might also want to know average miles per driver or average miles per week.

EXERCISE 3: FINDING AVERAGES

▶ The table below shows total miles driven over a 5-week period by different drivers of a moving company. Calculate total miles for each week and for each driver. Then calculate the average miles per week and the average miles per driver. If you find the totals first, you can then use constant divisors to find average miles per week and miles per driver. Set decimal for whole numbers.

Driver	Week 1	2	3	4	5	Total	Average Miles per Week
A	1,452	1,209	2,043	1,344	1,821	_____	_____
B	2,317	1,698	1,872	1,302	2,007	_____	_____
C	985	1,564	1,027	872	1,289	_____	_____
D	2,130	2,340	2,143	1,876	2,030	_____	_____
E	1,924	1,433	1,259	2,271	981	_____	_____
F	721	850	931	1,023	714	_____	_____
Total	____	____	____	____	____		
Average Miles per Driver	____	____	____	____	____		

▶ The moving company also keeps records and averages about the weekly salaries drivers receive. This varies based on the number of hours worked, the rate of pay, and overtime. Calculate the totals and averages for the following drivers and weeks to two decimal places (dollars and cents).

Driver	Week 1	2	3	4	5	Total	Average Salary per Week
A	546.63	313.34	612.90	362.87	518.99	_____	_____
B	637.18	448.27	436.18	367.95	527.84	_____	_____
C	365.86	516.12	363.81	377.50	451.15	_____	_____
D	601.09	620.55	561.63	475.38	581.04	_____	_____
E	555.37	391.78	361.18	676.30	392.67	_____	_____
F	252.35	348.01	299.75	387.73	265.40	_____	_____
Total	_____	____	____	____	____		
Average Salary per Driver	____	____	____	____	____		

Lesson 7
APPLY YOUR SKILLS

▶ Calculate the following weekly wages based on the stated hourly rate. Set the decimal selector at 2. If you have a constant function, set it at K. Use the constant function for speed and accuracy.

1. Hourly rate: $5.35			2. Hourly rate: $6.37		
Employee	Hours	Wages	Employee	Hours	Wages
Avery	35	_____	Kiteridge	39	_____
Bourbaki	27.5	_____	Lamont	37.5	_____
Clinton	38	_____	Murphy	34.5	_____
Day	33.5	_____	Nunio	29	_____
Estevez	36	_____	Obermeier	36.5	_____
Florio	28.5	_____	Parsky	34	_____
Gomez	40	_____	Quinn	38	_____
Havel	36.5	_____	Romero	39.5	_____
Itaki	40	_____	Shumacher	37.5	_____
Joyce	34.5	_____	Turner	35.5	_____

▶ Calculate the following wages at the given rates. Note that these are not weekly wages.

3. Hourly rate: $11.46			4. Hourly rate: $14.73		
Employee	Hours	Wages	Employee	Hours	Wages
Austin	140	_____	Quigley	112.5	_____
Cesnarsky	96.5	_____	Rollie	119	_____
Everett	135	_____	Samson	120	_____
Fiengo	113	_____	Truehart	84.5	_____
Garvey	154	_____	Unser	147.5	_____
Humbert	139.5	_____	Vanoth	128	_____
Inrak	156.5	_____	Welsh	131.5	_____
Jones	124.5	_____	Wexler	145	_____
Kresky	98	_____	Yankovich	136.5	_____
Lambert	108.5	_____	Zogby	157	_____

Name _____

Lesson 7
CHECK YOUR PROGRESS

▶ Find the following products and quotients, and then add the answers to find the total of each column. Use the constant function as needed. Round each answer to two places.

1. 3.45 x 18 = _____   2. 87 ÷ 6.3   = _____

3. 3.45 x 45 = _____   4. 5.67 ÷ 6.3 = _____

5. 3.45 x 76 = _____   6. 25.4 ÷ 6.3 = _____

7. 3.45 x 91 = _____   8. 94 ÷ 6.3   = _____

9. 3.45 x 56 = _____   10. 49.08 ÷ 6.3 = _____

        Total _____   Total _____

▶ Find the weekly wages for each of the following employees.

11. Hourly rate: $7.05

Employee	Hours	Wages
Adikes	25	_____
Burns	37.5	_____
Crom	18.5	_____
Fernandez	30.5	_____

12. Hourly rate: $6.17

Employee	Hours	Wages
Hu-Li	17	_____
Ister	27.5	_____
Jansky	14.5	_____
Kelly	10	_____

Name _____

Lesson 7
MASTERY CHECKPOINT

▶ Find the following products, and then add the products to find the total of each column. Use the constant key as needed. Round each answer to two places

1. 6.548 x 34 = _____   2. 7.09 x 3.45 = _____

3. 6.548 x 96 = _____   4. 7.09 x 34.7 = _____

5. 6.548 x 17 = _____   6. 7.09 x 65.2 = _____

7. 6.548 x 65 = _____   8. 7.09 x 45.8 = _____

9. 6.548 x 71 = _____   10. 7.09 x 38.9 = _____

            Total _____   Total _____

▶ For the following table, find the total miles, total gallons, average miles per day, average gallons per day, and total miles per gallon.

	Mon.	Tues.	Wed.	Thurs.	Fri.	Total	Average
Miles	459	401	123	398	376	11. _____	12. _____
Gallons	40.3	39.7	11.8	38.5	37.9	13. _____	14. _____

15. Miles per gallon _____

LESSON

USE OF THE MEMORY KEYS

OBJECTIVES

After completing this lesson, you will be able to:

- Use the memory keys to add, subtract, and recall amounts in memory.
- Use the memory keys in solving business math problems.

MEMORY AND ADDITION

It often happens that business math problems have several parts. For example, in working out payroll it might be necessary to calculate the wages for a number of different employees and then add these together to find the total payroll expense.

The memory keys on business calculators allow you to save the results of calculations and use them later. The memory keys vary with different calculator models. Some of the common keys are $\boxed{M+}$ and $\boxed{+I}$ for adding to memory, $\boxed{M-}$ and $\boxed{-I}$ for subtracting from memory, $\boxed{M\diamond}$ and $\boxed{I\diamond}$ for recalling and showing what is in memory. $\boxed{M*}$ or $\boxed{*I}$ are used to show the total amount in memory and then clear the memory. In the examples, we give general directions for the steps to be followed, but the exact keys and key strokes can vary. Review the use of memory in the manual that accompanies your calculator.

DEMONSTRATION EXAMPLE 1

Perform the indicated operations. Use the memory keys to store in memory and to recall your final answer: (3 x 4.76) + (7 x 3.11)

1. Clear memory
2. Multiply 3 x 4.76
3. Enter the product in memory. Display is 14.28
4. Multiply 7 x 3.11
5. Enter the product in memory. Display is 21.77
6. Recall the amount from memory. Display is 36.05

EXERCISE 1: USING MEMORY TO ADD WHOLE NUMBERS

▶ For each exercise: Find the first product and enter it in memory. Then find the second product and enter it in memory. Then recall the total from memory to find the answer. Set the decimal indicator at 0.

1. (15 x 325) + (63 x 709)
2. (67 x 300) + (80 x 135)
3. (21 x 471) + (40 x 300)
4. (59 x 798) + (76 x 867)
5. (41 x 368) + (17 x 717)
6. (732 x 519) + (411 x 803)
7. (612 x 403) + (899 x 376)
8. (867 x 211) + (761 x 101)
9. (452 x 610) + (901 x 901)
10. (580 x 508) + (420 x 204)

DEMONSTRATION EXAMPLE 2

Calculate (45 x $7.15) + (73 x $4.95) using memory keys.

First clear memory. Set the decimal selector at 2.

Enter 45 x 7.15	Display is 321.75
Add the result to memory.	
Enter 73 x 4.95	Display is 361.35
Add the result to memory.	
Recall the amount in memory.	Display is 683.10

1. USING MEMORY TO ADD WHOLE NUMBERS

1. _____
2. _____
3. _____
4. _____
5. _____
6. _____
7. _____
8. _____
9. _____
10. _____

Name _____

2. USING MEMORY TO ADD DECIMALS

1. _____

2. _____

3. _____

4. _____

5. _____

▶ In the following exercises, again use the memory key to store each partial answer. Then use the recall memory to find the answer. Set your decimal indicator at 2.

1. (5 x 3.45) + (16 x 4.35)

2. (19 x 6.83) + (24 x 1.98) + (26 x 7.55)

3. (25 x 17.44) + (46 x 24.68) + (78 x 18.80)

4. (30 x 19.80) + (67 x 7.05) + (44 x 23.40)

5. (24 x 38.75) + (17 x 45.25) + (20 x 15.49)

MEMORY AND SUBTRACTION

Numbers can be subtracted from the amount stored in memory in a way similar to that used for adding to memory. Set the decimal selector at 2.

DEMONSTRATION EXAMPLE 3

Use the memory add and subtract keys as needed. Set the decimal selector at 2.

(45 x 8.7) – 164.3 – (309 ÷ 24)

Enter 45 x 8.7	Display is 391.5
Add the amount to memory.	
Enter 164.3	Display is 164.3
Subtract the amount from memory.	
Enter 309 ÷ 24	Display is 12.88
Subtract the amount from memory.	
Recall the amount in memory.	Display is 214.32

EXERCISE 3: USING MEMORY TO SUBTRACT

▶ Use your memory add and subtract keys as needed and the memory recall to find answers to the following. Some of the exercises use division. Set your decimal selector at 2.

1. $(34 \times 15) - (13 \times 29)$

2. $(2{,}318 \div 9) - (14 \times 5.6)$

3. $(419 \times 2.7) + (68 \div 4)$

4. $(26 \times 11.2) - (506 \div 30.5)$

5. $(12 \times 7.4) + (35 \div 6.3)$

6. $(14.3 \times 9.4) - (4.5 \times 9) + (42 \times 1.6)$

7. $(74 \times 6.5) - (78.4 \div 5) - (4.3 \times 7.2)$

8. $(102 \times 6) + (456 \div 16) - (3{,}045 \div 85)$

9. $(76.5 \times 3) - (24.8 \times 6) - (301 \div 7)$

10. $(46 \times 3.5) + (14.5 \times 11) - (141 \div 17)$

11. $(3{,}040 \div 45) - (3{,}672 \div 60) + 211.8$

12. $(31.8 \times 56.9) - 907.5 - (21 \times 6.4)$

13. $(45.9 \div 6) + (204 \div 12.5) - (325 \div 29)$

14. $(10.5 \times 27) - (3.9 \times 3.8) - (25 \times 2.7)$

15. $(302 \times 0.6) - 98.4 - (56 \times 0.3)$

1. _____

2. _____

3. _____

4. _____

5. _____

6. _____

7. _____

8. _____

9. _____

10. _____

11. _____

12. _____

13. _____

14. _____

15. _____

Name _____

Lesson 8
APPLY YOUR SKILLS

▶ Calculate extensions for the following partial invoices. Use the memory in order to find the totals. Set the decimal selector at 2.

CONSUMER PRODUCTS INC.			
QUANTITY	**ITEM**	**UNIT PRICE**	**AMOUNT**
20 tubes	Toothpaste	$ 1.95 ea	1. _____
60	Razors	4.29 ea	2. _____
12 doz	Combs	1.45 a doz	3. _____
75 containers	Vitamins	3.60 ea	4. _____
15 doz	Pens	2.88 a doz	5. _____
8 boxes	Notebooks	24.75 a box	6. _____
		Total	7. _____

BOOKS GALORE			
85 copies	Cooking for Fun	14.95 ea	8. _____
72 copies	Gardening	9.62 ea	9. _____
60 copies	Macrame	6.50 ea	10. _____
94 copies	How to Compute	8.38 ea	11. _____
78 copies	Dining Out	12.60 ea	12. _____
150 copies	Exercising at Home	7.95 ea	13. _____
		Total	14. _____

B & C FOOD STORE			
12 cases	Canned tomatoes	23.60 a case	15. _____
65 cases	Club soda	13.76 a case	16. _____
20 boxes	Corn flakes	19.65 a box	17. _____
85 pounds	Potatoes	0.45 a lb	18. _____
70 pounds	Carrots	0.29 a lb	19. _____
		Total	20. _____

Name _____

Lesson 8
APPLY YOUR SKILLS (continued)

▶ Use the constant function to calculate the wages for each individual. Enter each amount in memory so that you can find the grand total.

21. Hourly rate: $9.35

Employee	Hours	Wages
Avery	85	_____
Bourbaki	77.5	_____
Clinton	78	_____
Day	53.5	_____
Estevez	96	_____
Florio	68.5	_____
Gomez	90	_____
Havel	58.5	_____
Itaki	75	_____
Joyce	84.5	_____
Total		_____

22. Hourly rate: $12.37

Employee	Hours	Wages
Kiteridge	99	_____
Lamont	97.5	_____
Murphy	84.5	_____
Nunio	68	_____
Obermeier	73	_____
Parsky	64	_____
Quinn	98	_____
Romero	79.5	_____
Shumacher	77.5	_____
Turner	65	_____
Total		_____

▶ Calculate the following wages and totals at the given rates.

23. Hourly rate: $8.46

Employee	Hours	Wages
Austin	150	_____
Cesnarsky	86.5	_____
Everett	145	_____
Fiengo	133	_____
Garvey	154	_____
Humbert	148.5	_____
Inrak	156.5	_____
Jones	124.5	_____
Kresky	98	_____
Lambert	108.5	_____
Total		_____

24. Hourly rate: $15.43

Employee	Hours	Wages
Quigley	125	_____
Rollie	109.5	_____
Samson	140.5	_____
Truehart	94.5	_____
Unser	107.5	_____
Vanoth	148.5	_____
Welsh	162.5	_____
Wexler	155	_____
Yankovich	146.5	_____
Zogby	137	_____
Total		_____

Lesson 8
CHECK YOUR PROGRESS

▶ Use the calculator memory in finding each answer.

1. $(45 \times 3.4) + (15.2 \times 14) =$ _____

2. $(87 \times 2.5) - (16 \times 5.2) =$ _____

3. $(317 " 21) + (21.7 \times 9) - (504 " 23) =$ _____

4. $(73 \times 11.4) - 402.8 + (3 \times 54) =$ _____

5. $(210 " 3.5) - (99 \times 0.6) + 0.5 =$ _____

▶ Calculate the extensions and total for the partial book store invoice.

25 copies	The Civil War	24.95 ea	6. _____
40 copies	The Last Winter	9.62 ea	7. _____
52 copies	Lincoln	6.50 ea	8. _____
18 copies	Math for Fun	8.38 ea	9. _____
35 copies	Carpentry	12.60 ea	10. _____
		Total	_____

Name _____

Lesson 8
MASTERY CHECKPOINT

▶ Use the calculator memory in finding each answer.

1. (80 x 3.4) + (2.5 x 37) =   _____
2. (150 " 2.4) – (3.8 x 9.6) =   _____
3. (504 " 21) – (56 " 4.5) – (12 x 0.8) =   _____
4. (13 x 6.5) + (7 x 29.4) – 102.6 =   _____
5. (80 x 1.2) – 24 – (23.6 x 1.6) =   _____

▶ Use the constant function to calculate the wages for each individual. Enter each amount in memory so that you can find the grand total.

6. Hourly rate: $7.64

Employee	Hours	Wages
Arnold	75	_____
Belter	77.5	_____
Clark	78	_____
Duffy	53.5	_____
Elmont	96	_____
Total		_____

7. Hourly rate: $14.80

Employee	Hours	Wages
Kiteridge	99	_____
Li	97.5	_____
Munez	84.5	_____
Polk	68	_____
Quinlin	73	_____
Total		_____

PETTY CASH AND BANKING

OBJECTIVES

After completing this lesson you will be able to:

- Correctly enter and total transactions in a petty cash book.
- Correctly enter transactions in a business checking account.

RECORDING SMALL EXPENSES

You may think of business expenses as large expenditures, such as money spent for salaries, equipment, and merchandise to sell. But businesses also have many small expenses. These must be carefully recorded so that money is not lost or misplaced and so that the company will know exactly how it is spending money.

Companies keep petty cash books or computerized spreadsheets to record small expenses. The clerk responsible for this book writes out a voucher for each petty cash transaction. The voucher is a slip that shows the amount disbursed, the purpose of the disbursement, and the date. It is signed by the person receiving the money and by the petty cash clerk. The petty cash clerk then records the amount in the petty cash book.

A partial page from a petty cash spreadsheet is shown in Figure 9.1. At the beginning of the month, the petty cash clerk has $800, the amount received. Each entry after that records an amount paid out. Each amount is recorded twice: once in the "paid out" column and again in an expense column (Office Exp., Delivery, or Misc.). "Brought forward (Brought f'wd)," refers to the amount that came from the previous page of the cash record book.

When all accounts are totaled at the end of a month, the total in the Paid Out column is subtracted from the Amount Received at the start of the month. The difference is called Cash on Hand:

Amount Received – Amount Paid Out = Cash on Hand

	1	2	3	4	5	6	7	8
1	Received	Paid out	Date	Explanation	No.	Office Exp.	Delivery	Misc.
2	800.00		6/1	Company Ck.				
3		412.27	6/20	Brought f'wd				
4		48.10	6/24	Comp Paper	223	48.10		
5								

Figure 9.1.   Partial page from a petty cash spreadsheet

EXERCISE 1: USING PETTY CASH SPREADSHEETS

▶ Find the totals for each column and the cash on hand at the end of the month for the following transactions in the petty cash book.

1.

	1	2	3	4	5	6	7	8
	Received	Paid out	Date	Explanation	No.	Office Exp.	Delivery	Misc.
1								
2	800.00		6/1	Company Ck.				
3		412.27	6/20	Brought f'wd				
4		48.10	6/24	Comp. Paper	223	48.10		
5		93.24	6/25	Disks	224	93.24		
6		9.50	6/28	Express Mail	225		9.50	
7		15.50	6/29	Fax	226		15.50	
8		10.50	6/30	Taxi	227		10.50	
9		17.88	6/31	Pens/pencils	228	17.88		
10				TOTALS				

Figure 9.2. Petty cash spreadsheet for transaction 1

Cash on Hand _____

2.

	1	2	3	4	5	6	7	8
	Received	Paid out	Date	Explanation	No.	Office Exp.	Delivery	Misc.
1								
2	700.00		7/1	Company Ck.				
3		541.08	7/22	Brought f'wd				
4		57.91	7/22	Copying	311	57.91		
5		19.84	7/23	Disks	312	19.84		
6		17.50	7/26	Express Mail	313		17.50	
7		33.78	7/28	Bus. Lunch	314			33.78
8		23.00	6/29	Fax	315		23.00	
9		7.86	6/30	Batteries	316	7.86		
10				TOTALS				

Figure 9.3. Petty cash spreadsheet for transaction 2

Cash on Hand _____

Name _____

EXERCISE 2: ENTERING TRANSACTIONS

▶ Enter transactions for exercise 1 on Figure 9.4. Enter transactions for exercise 2 on Figure 9.5. Then find the totals and cash on hand for each. Start voucher numbers at 401 for transaction 1 and 501 for transaction 2. Determine the most appropriate expense category for each item. Abbreviate when necessary.

1. 9/1   Received, $800
    Paid out
      9/3   Computer paper, $74.58
      9/5   Express mail, $21.50
      9/6   Software, $110.70
      9/9   Taxi, $16.50
      9/10   Lunch, $35.73
      9/12   Fax, $21.50

2. 10/1   Received, $700
    Paid out
      10/2   Copier cartridge, $115.67
      10/4   Delivery messenger, $14
      10/5   Computer disks, $97.24
      10/9   Postage, $78.66
      10/11 Plant for office, $11.95
      10/14 File folders, $18.79

	1	2	3	4	5	6	7	8
1	Received	Paid out	Date	Explanation	No.	Office Exp.	Delivery	Misc.
2								
3								
4								
5								
6								
7								
8								
9								
10								

Figure 9.4.   Petty cash spreadsheet for transaction 1

Cash on Hand _____

	1	2	3	4	5	6	7	8
1	Received	Paid out	Date	Explanation	No.	Office Exp.	Delivery	Misc.
2								
3								
4								
5								
6								
7								
8								
9								
10								

Figure 9.5.   Petty cash spreadsheet for transaction 2

Cash on Hand _____

EXERCISE 2: ENTERING TRANSACTIONS (continued)

▶ Enter transactions for exercise 3 on Figure 9.6. Enter transactions for exercise 4 on Figure 9.7. Then find the totals and final cash on hand. Start voucher numbers at 201 for transaction 3 and 301 for transaction 4. You decide on the expense category. Abbreviate when necessary.

3. 11/1   Received, $750
    Paid out
    11/1   Calculators, $98.56
    11/2   Stamps, $29
    11/5   Express Mail, $39.75
    11/8   Business lunch, $41.71
    11/9   Pencils and pens, $19.36
    11/12   Fax, $21
    11/14   Cups, $14.50

4. 12/1   Received, $500
    Paid out
    12/3   Copying, $44.20
    12/4   Postage, $114.56
    12/5   Computer ribbons, $56.39
    12/8   Lunch, $9.61
    12/9   Film development, $19.87
    12/11   Express Mail, $27.50
    12/14   Envelopes, $31.74

	1	2	3	4	5	6	7	8
1	Received	Paid out	Date	Explanation	No.	Office Exp.	Delivery	Misc.
2								
3								
4								
5								
6								
7								
8								
9								
10								

Figure 9.6.   Petty cash spreadsheet for transaction 3

Cash on Hand _____

	1	2	3	4	5	6	7	8
1	Received	Paid out	Date	Explanation	No.	Office Exp.	Delivery	Misc.
2								
3								
4								
5								
6								
7								
8								
9								
10								

Figure 9.7.   Petty cash spreadsheet for transaction 4

Cash on Hand _____

Name _____

CHECK REGISTER FOR A SMALL BUSINESS

You may be familiar with a personal checking account and the check register. Small businesses maintain checking accounts similar to those used by individuals. Each transaction is entered in the check register. Notice that a deposit is added to the previous balance, and the amount of each check is subtracted from the previous balance. The new balance is calculated by adding or subtracting the amount of each transaction from the previous balance.

The check register shown in Figure 9.8 contains several transactions and the balance as recorded after each transaction.

NUMBER	DATE	DESCRIPTION OF TRANSACTION	PAYMENT/DEBIT (−)	✔ T	FEE IF ANY (−)	DEPOSIT/CREDIT (+)	BALANCE	
							2000	00
	5/3	Weekly sales				950.25	2950	25
201	5/4	Rent	590.00				2360	25
202	5/5	Supplies	78.43				2281	82

Figure 9.8. Sample check register

EXERCISE 3: WORKING WITH CHECK REGISTERS

▶ Complete the balance for each transaction in the check register in Figure 9.9.

NUMBER	DATE	DESCRIPTION OF TRANSACTION	PAYMENT/DEBIT (−)	✓T	FEE IF ANY (−)	DEPOSIT/CREDIT (+)	BALANCE 1500 00	
301	6/1	Taxes	740.00					
	6/2	Sales				953.27		
	6/3	Salary	210.50					
	6/4	Supplies	94.63					

Figure 9.9.   Practice check register

Name _____

1. _____
2. _____
3. _____
4. _____
5. _____
6. _____
7. _____
8. _____
9. _____
10. _____
11. _____
12. _____
13. _____
14. _____
15. _____
16. _____
17. _____
18. _____
19. _____
20. _____
21. _____
22. _____
23. _____
24. _____
25. _____
26. _____
27. _____
28. _____
29. _____
30. _____

Lesson 9
TOUCH DRILL FOR SPEED DEVELOPMENT

▶ Record the total number of minutes and seconds it takes to complete these exercises on the line provided. Calculate each sum.

1. 789	2. 456	3. 213	4. 865
898	565	312	896
897	645	232	568
998	465	123	958

5. 25,412	6. 78,545	7. 23,565	8. 15,951
45,142	75,484	65,236	75,375
51,242	45,587	36,525	95,191
15,245	78,454	52,363	73,573

▶ Subtract.

9. 74,174	10. 85,285	11. 93,396	12. 76,143
−17,417	−19,595	−63,963	−93,175

13. 714,792	14. 985,208	15. 764,562	16. 789,674
−295,311	−871,612	−470,312	−262,295

▶ Divide. Set your decimal selector at 0.

17. $4,572 \div 52$ 18. $187,358 \div 41$

19. $761,198 \div 274$ 20. $1,644,672 \div 753$

21. $549,412 \div 638$ 22. $4,602,901 \div 867$

▶ Find the sum for each problem below. Set your decimal selector at A. Remember that each entry must be a two-place decimal.

23. 404.90	24. 708.83	25. 84.89	26. 74.57
934.87	158.62	704.08	331.02
78.64	273.65	12.84	168.45
57.53	128.40	398.07	839.05

27. 352.40	28. 807.08	29. 218.54	30. 705.41
619.12	421.00	874.33	75.21
580.06	89.09	763.29	467.32
5.02	656.89	8.78	771.48

Lesson 9
APPLY YOUR SKILLS

▶ Enter transactions for exercise 1 on Figure 9.10. Enter transactions for exercise 2 on Figure 9.11. Find the new balance after each transaction.

1.	7/1	Deposit $1,780, sales
	7/3	Pay $45.60, light bulbs
	7/4	Pay $119.87, repairs
	7/8	Pay $415.28, salary
	7/8	Deposit $2,031.25, sales
	7/9	Pay $341.62, furniture
	7/10	Pay $1,025.63, merchandise

2.	8/1	Deposit $1,546.93, sales
	8/1	Pay $509.87, salary
	8/2	Pay $134.27, supplies
	8/3	Pay $764.20, merchandise
	8/4	Deposit $1,287.41, sales

1.

NUMBER	DATE	DESCRIPTION OF TRANSACTION	PAYMENT/DEBIT (−)	✔T	FEE IF ANY (−)	DEPOSIT/CREDIT (+)	BALANCE	

Figure 9.10.   Check register for transaction 1

2.

NUMBER	DATE	DESCRIPTION OF TRANSACTION	PAYMENT/DEBIT (−)	✔T	FEE IF ANY (−)	DEPOSIT/CREDIT (+)	BALANCE	

Figure 9.11.   Check register for transaction 2

Name _____

Lesson 9
CHECK YOUR PROGRESS

▶ Enter the following petty cash transactions on Figure 9.12. Then find the totals and the cash on hand. Start voucher numbers at 201. Determine the most appropriate expense category. Abbreviate as needed.

9/1	Received, $900
Paid out	
9/1	Calculators, $45.78
9/3	Copying, $19.20
9/4	Fax, $18
9/5	Express mail, $23.00
9/8	Business lunch, $56.03
9/9	Fax, $21
9/10	Taxi, $12.35
	Computer ribbon, $9.19

	1	2	3	4	5	6	7	8
1	Received	Paid out	Date	Explanation	No.	Office Exp.	Delivery	Misc.
2								
3								
4								
5								
6								
7								
8								
9								
10								

Figure 9.12. Petty cash spreadsheet for Check Your Progress

Cash on Hand _____

Lesson 9
MASTERY CHECKPOINT

▶ Enter the following transactions in the check register (Figure 9.13) and find the new balance after each transaction.

4/1	Deposit $2,950, sales
4/2	Pay $65.40, supplies
4/3	Pay $650, rent
4/4	Pay $214.98, salary
4/5	Pay $605.27, taxes
4/9	Deposit $1,331.85, sales
4/10	Pay $256.09, software
4/11	Pay $94.55, repairs

NUMBER	DATE	DESCRIPTION OF TRANSACTION	PAYMENT/DEBIT (–)	✓T	FEE IF ANY (–)	DEPOSIT/CREDIT (+)	BALANCE	

Figure 9.13.   Check register for Mastery Checkpoint

Name _____

THE MEANING OF PERCENT

OBJECTIVES

After completing this lesson you will be able to:

- Convert among fractions, decimals, and percents.
- Find an amount, rate, or base when the other two are given.

CALCULATING A PERCENTAGE

A ratio is a way of expressing a relationship between two numbers. "5 out of every 7 dollars is spent on salaries." "3 out of 4 employees in the company earn more than $18,000." These ratios can easily be converted to decimal numbers. Percentages provide an easy, consistent way to express the relationship of one quantity to another.

To convert a ratio to a decimal, divide the numerator (top) by the denominator (bottom):

$$3/4 = 3 \div 4 = 0.75$$

Percent means parts out of 100. Saying that 50% of the people voted for Smith means that 50 out of every hundred, or half, voted for Smith. Since a two-place decimal means hundredths, such decimals can be converted to percents by simply moving the decimal point two places to the right.

$$0.25 = 25\%$$

Since any fraction can be converted to a two-place decimal, fractions can be converted to percents. First convert the fraction to a two-place decimal. Then convert the decimal to a percent.

The grid in Figure 10.1 shows 100 small squares. 25 of these are shaded. 25 out of 100 means 1/4 or 0.25 or 25%.

Figure 10.1. Grid illustrating 25 percent

The basic formula for calculating a percentage is:

Amount = Base x Rate

Rate means percent, that is, the number with the percent sign. This formula is also used for calculating base, or rate, when the other two are known. The triangle in Figure 10.2 can help you remember the relationships.

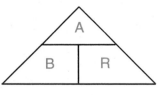

Figure 10.2. Triangle model for working with percents

The base is the total amount, equal to 100%. The rate is the percent of that total. The amount is the result of multiplying the base by the rate. It is a portion of the base. Base and rate are side by side in the triangle. They are multiplied to find the amount. Amount is over base. It is divided by the base to find the rate. Amount is also over rate. It is divided by the rate to find the base.

FINDING THE AMOUNT

DEMONSTRATION EXAMPLE 1

Find 22% of 729

In the triangle diagram (Figure 10.3), A is circled. This is what we want to find. Rate is next to base. These are multiplied. Pressing the $\boxed{\%}$ key after the multiplier gives the answer as a percent.

Amount	=	Base x Rate				
A	=	B x R				
	=	729 x 22%	Enter	729	x	22 %
			Display	729 729		22 160.38

22% of 729 is 160.38

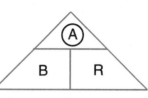

Figure 10.3   Triangle model for finding the amount

DEMONSTRATION EXAMPLE 2

Find 110% of 345

$$A = B \times R$$
$$A = 345 \times 110\% = 379.5$$

You have seen that the way to convert a fraction to a decimal is simply to divide the numerator by the denominator and then round the answer to two places. You can convert a decimal to a percent by moving the decimal point two places to the right and adding a percent sign.

28% means 28 parts out of 100: 28% = 28/100 = 0.28

A percent can be converted to a decimal by inserting a decimal point and then moving it two places to the left. A percent can be converted to a fraction by placing the percent over 100 and then reducing the fraction to its lowest terms.

DEMONSTRATION EXAMPLE 3

Convert 67% to a decimal.
There are two ways of thinking about this:

(1)   67% = 67/100 = 0.67

(2)   67.0% = 0.67 Moving the decimal point two places to the left.

DEMONSTRATION EXAMPLE 4

Convert 20% to a fraction and to a decimal.
20% = 20/100 = 1/5
20% = 0.2

EXERCISE 1: CONVERTING FRACTIONS, DECIMALS, PERCENTS

The following table shows conversions among fractions, decimals, and percents. Complete the table by finding the two that are missing in each row. Round decimals to the nearest hundredth. Find percents to the nearest whole number.

Fraction	Decimal	Percent
1/2		
	0.10	
		5%
	0.75	
2/3		
		30%
1/8		
	0.01	
		90%
	0.005	
2/7		
	1.2	
		150%
3/20		
		3%

DEMONSTRATION EXAMPLE 5

What is 45.6% of 673.4

673.4 x 45.6% = 307.07   Enter the base first for fewer key strokes.

2. DETERMINING THE AMOUNT

1. _____
2. _____
3. _____
4. _____
5. _____
6. _____
7. _____
8. _____
9. _____
10. _____
11. _____
12. _____
13. _____
14. _____
15. _____
16. _____
17. _____
18. _____
19. _____
20. _____
21. _____
22. _____
23. _____
24. _____
25. _____
26. _____

EXERCISE 2: DETERMINING THE AMOUNT

▶ Set the decimal high enough to enter all the numbers in the exercises. Set the decimal at 2 and use the percent (P or %) key to find the amounts.

1. What is 8% of 54?
2. What is 14% of 75.3?
3. What is 28.64% of 84.37?
4. What is 34.09% of 101?
5. What is 48.06% of 118.92?
6. What is 57.13% of 127.83?
7. What is 61.8% of 138.69?
8. What is 76.4% of 159.37?
9. What is 81.3% of 179.38?
10. What is 94.6% of 184.52?
11. What is 97.64% of 218.67?
12. What is 108% of 276.48?
13. What is 125% of 513.79?
14. What is 143.5% of 764.38?
15. What is 216.35% of 881.37?
16. What is 94.32% of 1,617.44?
17. What is 114.59% of 3,865.22?
18. What is 10.44% of 499.65?
19. What is 82.99% of 998.45?
20. What is 94% of 433?
21. What is 15.5% of 74?
22. What is 5.25% of 306?
23. What is 200% of 25.6?
24. What is 4.5% of 95?
25. What is 82.5% of 482?
26. What is 19% of 1,000?

Name _____

FINDING THE RATE

When you are asked, "48 is what percent of 200?" you are looking for the rate. If you draw the triangle as shown in Figure 10.2, you will be reminded that to find the rate you divide the amount by the base. When dividing to find the rate, remember that you must convert the decimal to a percent.

$$\text{Rate} = \frac{\text{Amount}}{\text{Base}} = \frac{48}{200}$$

$$= 0.24 = 24\%$$

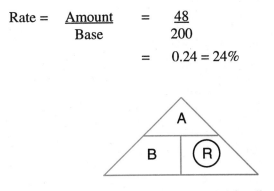

Figure 10.4.   Triangle model for finding the rate

DEMONSTRATION EXAMPLE

98.76 is what percent of 395.21?

In the triangle diagram (Figure 10.4), R is circled. We are looking for the rate. A is over B. Therefore the amount is divided by the base.

$$\text{Rate} = \frac{\text{Amount}}{\text{Base}}$$

$$= \frac{98.76}{395.21}$$

Enter	98.76	÷	395.21	
Display	98.76	98.76	395.21	0.2499

98.76 is 24.99% of 395.21

3. DETERMINING THE RATE

1. _____
2. _____
3. _____
4. _____
5. _____
6. _____
7. _____
8. _____
9. _____
10. _____
11. _____
12. _____
13. _____
14. _____
15. _____
16. _____
17. _____
18. _____
19. _____
20. _____

EXERCISE 3: DETERMINING THE RATE

▶ Set your calculator at 4 decimal places and determine the rate for the problems below.

1. 129.50 is what percent of 469?
2. 49 is what percent of 102?
3. 83.16 is what percent of 91.14?
4. 29.01 is what percent of 35.76?
5. 62.07 is what percent of 75.39?
6. 106.57 is what percent of 194.53?
7. 153.79 is what percent of 188.92?
8. 246.38 is what percent of 461.73?
9. 312.65 is what percent of 313.46?
10. 498.21is what percent of 426.81?
11. 362.49 is what percent of 335.81?
12. 1,806.74 is what percent of 335.26?
13. 6,500 is what percent of 7,945.31?
14. 7,352.60 is what percent of 10,490.50?
15. 1,013.25 is what percent of 1,506.81?
16. What percent is 62.50 of 884.9?
17. What percent is 99.95 of 77.60?
18. What percent is 49.95 of 298.80?
19. What percent is 101 of 141.02?
20. What percent is 212.67 of 106.33?

FINDING THE BASE

To find the base, you must divide the amount by the rate. Again, the triangle can be helpful. Amount (portion of the total) is over rate (percent), so amount must be divided by percent.

DEMONSTRATION EXAMPLE 1

75 is 25% of what number?

Base $= \dfrac{\text{Amount}}{\text{Rate}}$

Enter	75	÷	25	%
Display	75	75	25	300

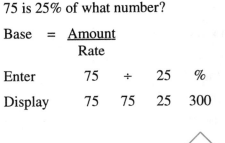

Figure 10.5   Triangle model for finding the base

DEMONSTRATION EXAMPLE 2

76 is 125% of what number?

Base $= \dfrac{\text{Amount}}{\text{Rate}}$

Base $=$ 76   ÷   125% $=$ 60.8

4. DETERMINING THE BASE

1. _____
2. _____
3. _____
4. _____
5. _____
6. _____
7. _____
8. _____
9. _____
10. _____
11. _____
12. _____
13. _____
14. _____
15. _____
16. _____
17. _____
18. _____
19. _____
20. _____

EXERCISE 4: DETERMINING THE BASE

 In each problem, find the base.

1. 19 is 33% of what number?
2. 43 is 24% of what number?
3. 64.2 is 37% of what number?
4. 73.4 is 45.1% of what number?
5. 82.46 is 67.1% of what number?
6. 109.67 is 89.4% of what number?
7. 125.94 is 105% of what number?
8. 273.49 is 118.6% of what number?
9. 346.78 is 142.6% of what number?
10. 671.83 is 64.8% of what number?
11. 1,256.78 is 74.5% of what number?
12. 1,596.27 is 102.8% of what number?
13. 1,973.46 is 97.1% of what number?
14. 8,219.73 is 106.5% of what number?
15. 10,749.53 is 99.5% of what number?
16. 106.75 is 45% of what number?
17. 555.62 is 98.6% of what number?
18. 7,342 is 81% of what number?
19. 170.75 is 69.4% of what number?
20. 17.48 is 23.59% of what number?

Lesson 10
TOUCH DRILL FOR SPEED DEVELOPMENT

▶ Calculate each sum. Record the total number of minutes and seconds it takes to complete these exercises on the line provided.

1.	2.	3.	4.
132	963	714	852
112	363	147	585
323	369	471	528
121	939	171	828

5.	6.	7.	8.
24,512	73,575	89,569	45,656
25,122	73,537	69,566	12,321
14,152	15,591	45,121	78,978
25,442	91,591	21,254	13,213

▶ Subtract.

9.	10.	11.	12.
44,174	45,654	89,798	65,263
−85,848	−35,753	−13,232	−12,542

13.	14.	15.	16.
784,102	784,671	506,812	780,302
−254,871	−456,102	−470,312	−670,230

▶ Divide. Set your decimal selector at 0.

17. $87,091 \div 50$ 18. $20,098 \div 40$

19. $904,720 \div 204$ 20. $809,670 \div 700$

21. $201,703 \div 308$ 22. $7,090,670 \div 809$

▶ Find the sum for each problem below. Set your decimal selector at A. Remember that each entry must be a two-place decimal.

23.	24.	25.	26.
560.00	640.21	18.90	85.30
501.26	189.38	640.90	300.05
8.09	893.10	50.00	340.10
78.02	681.20	129.04	185.00

27.	28.	29.	30.
581.02	172.33	589.00	904.00
478.00	478.09	126.30	67.11
345.67	60.00	564.00	180.20
89.01	109.04	48.50	459.07

TIME _____

TOUCH DRILL FOR SPEED DEVELOPMENT

1. _____
2. _____
3. _____
4. _____
5. _____
6. _____
7. _____
8. _____
9. _____
10. _____
11. _____
12. _____
13. _____
14. _____
15. _____
16. _____
17. _____
18. _____
19. _____
20. _____
21. _____
22. _____
23. _____
24. _____
25. _____
26. _____
27. _____
28. _____
29. _____
30. _____

Name _____

1. _____

2. _____

3. _____

4. _____

5. _____

6. _____

7. _____

8. _____

9. _____

10. _____

11. A_____

   B_____

12. _____

Lesson 10
APPLY YOUR SKILLS

▶ Read each problem. Decide whether you are looking for the amount, rate, or base. Set up the equation for multiplication or division. Work out the problem. Check to see that your answer is reasonable.

1. A person invests 24% of $6,200. How much does she invest?

   _____

2. A person spent $450 out of $9,000. What percent does he spend?

   _____

3. A person receives $50. This is 20% of what a second person receives. How much does the second person receive?

   _____

4. An owner rents 87% of a building with 20,000 square feet of space. How many square feet does she rent?

   _____

5. A person receives $340 out of $1000. What percent of the total does he receive?

   _____

6. Company A pays $20,000 for 3.5% of Company B. How much would Company A pay for all of Company B?

   _____

7. A person put 16% of $468.90 in the bank. How much does he put in the bank?

   _____

8. Company X pays $1 million for part ownership of Company Y. If Company Y is valued at $5 million, what percent of Y is owned by X?

   _____

9. Mr. X invests $40,000 in a partnership worth $1 million. What percent of the total amount comes from Mr. X?

   _____

10. Ms. A takes out 15% of the money she had in the bank. If she takes out $75, how much did she have in the bank?

   _____

11. Person A contributes $450 and Person B contributes $550 to a charity that collects a total of $6,000. What percent of the total does each person contribute?

   A _____
   B _____

12. Company D sells 22% of its stock to Company E. There are 65,400 shares of stock in all. How many does Company E buy?

   _____

Lesson 10
CHECK YOUR PROGRESS

▶ The following are mixed exercises in which you are asked to find the amount (portion of the total), base (the total), or rate (percent). Read each exercise carefully. Check your answers to see that they make sense. Remember the rate can be greater than 100%.

1. Find 25% of $402.30.

2. Find 6% of $46.50.

3. 6 is 40% of what number?

4. $4 is 20% of what amount?

5. 7 is what percent of 50?

6. 8.4 is what percent of 45?

7. 7.3 is 15% of what number?

8. What is 6.3% of $502?

9. $11 is what percent of $200?

10. 88 is what percent of 40?

11. 93 is 200% of what number?

12. Find 200% of 65.4.

13. If Ms. X receives a payment of $83.50 out of $900, what percent has she received?

14. Mr. A pays a 20% deposit on an item costing $456. How much is the deposit?

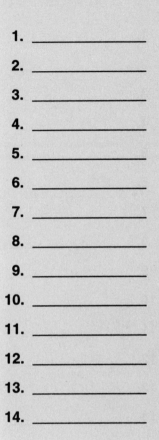

CHECK YOUR PROGRESS

1. _____
2. _____
3. _____
4. _____
5. _____
6. _____
7. _____
8. _____
9. _____
10. _____
11. _____
12. _____
13. _____
14. _____

Name _____

Lesson 10
MASTERY CHECKPOINT

1. _____

2. _____

3. _____

4. _____

5. _____

6. _____

7. _____

8. _____

9. _____

10. _____

11. _____

12. _____

13. _____

14. _____

▶ Find each percentage, rate, or base.

1. $3 is what percent of $9?

2. 70 is what percent of 30?

3. Find 4.5% of $801.

4. $4.57 is what percent of $10?

5. Find 22.3% of $607.

6. $60 is 110% of what amount?

7. $3.25 is 6% of what amount?

8. Find 2.5% of $734.67.

9. 6 is what percent of 7?

10. 7 is what percent of 6?

11. What is 5.5% of $402?

12. $6 is 40% of what amount?

13. If two people divide $8,500 so that one receives 40%, how much money does the other receive?

14. If Company A buys 31% of Company B for $3.4 million, how much would Company A have to pay for the whole company?

DISCOUNT

After completing this lesson you will be able to:

- Find a discount amount and net cost.
- Correctly calculate discounts based on payment terms.

DETERMINING DISCOUNTS

Everyone likes to buy something on sale. We believe that we have saved money when a jacket or pair of shoes or tape player can be purchased for less than the usual price.

People and companies selling merchandise offer discounts for several reasons: (1) to reward a customer for making a large purchase; (2) to reward a customer for paying promptly; (3) to lower a selling price as an incentive to purchase. Discounts are usually based on a percent of the selling price. For example, a discount of 10% on an item selling for $200 will mean a reduction in price of $20.

DEMONSTRATION EXAMPLE

Retail cost: $1,250.00

Discount rate: 7%

Discount amount	=	Retail cost x Discount rate
	=	1,250 x 7%
	=	87.50
Net cost	=	Retail cost – Discount amount
	=	1,250 – 87.50
	=	1,162.50

Note the following vocabulary. *List price* means the original price; price charged a retail customer. *Discount* is a deduction from the retail cost. *Discount rate* is a percent of retail cost deducted for prompt payment, quantity purchase, or some other reason. *Discount amount* means an amount deducted from the retail cost. *Net cost* is the actual cost to buyer after discount is deducted from retail cost.

EXERCISE 1: FINDING THE DISCOUNT AMOUNT AND NET COST

▶ Find the discount amount and net cost. Set the decimal selector at 2. Convert fractional percents to decimals; for example, 4 1/2% = 4.5%.

	List Price	Discount Rate	Discount Amount	Net Cost
1.	435	4%	_____	_____
2.	863	7 1/2%	_____	_____
3.	649	10%	_____	_____
4.	127	6 1/2%	_____	_____
5.	1,821	2%	_____	_____

Name_____

DISCOUNT TERMS

The top of an invoice often includes a box marked "terms." In this box are indicated the discount terms for payment within specified times. These terms are incentives for the purchaser to pay as quickly as possible. The following are a few such terms and what they mean.

3/10 A 3% discount is given if payment is made in 10 days or less.

2/20 A 2% discount is given if payment is made in 20 days or less.

N/30 The invoice must be paid within 30 days. After 30 days there may be a finance charge. N stands for the net amount, that is, the invoice total with no discount.

Sometimes an invoice will show several discounts, for example: 3/10, 2/20.

This means that a 3% discount is given for payment in 10 days or less, and a 2% discount is given for payment from 11 to 20 days.

DEMONSTRATION EXAMPLE

Find each discount and total after the discount is subtracted.

Amount $456.30; terms 4/15; payment was made in 10 days.

Payment is made within the terms of the 4% discount.

456.30 x 4%   = 18.25

456.30 – 18.25 = 438.05

Amount $715.93; terms 3/10, 2/20; payment was made in 14 days.

Payment is made within the terms of the 2% discount.

715.93 x 2% = 14.32

715.93 – 14.32 = 701.61

EXERCISE 2: WORKING WITH DISCOUNT TERMS

▶ Find the discount and total to be paid for each of the following.

	Amount	Terms	When Paid	Discount	Total
1.	$892.16	3/15	12 days	_____	_____
2.	$304.50	3/15	18 days	_____	_____
3.	$612.44	3/10, 2/20	8 days	_____	_____
4.	$940.28	3/10, 2/30	22 days	_____	_____
5.	$2,308.76	2/10, N/30	9 days	_____	_____
6.	$1,904.36	3/10, 1/30	12 days	_____	_____
7.	$3,412.05	4/10, 3/20	15 days	_____	_____
8.	$4,902.20	4/10, 3/20	2 days	_____	_____
9.	$6,209.56	3/10, N/30	22 days	_____	_____
10.	$783.29	3/10, N/30	4 days	_____	_____

SALES TAX

In some places, a state or local sales tax must be added to the selling price. This sales tax is a percent of the invoice amount after any discount is taken. Companies and stores must keep careful records of sales tax collections and pay the amounts to the state or local government at given intervals—usually every three months.

DEMONSTRATION EXAMPLE 1

Find the total for an invoice of $517.83 with a 4.5% sales tax.

517.83 x 4.5% = 23.30

517.83 + 23.30 = 541.13

DEMONSTRATION EXAMPLE 2

The calculations required to complete the invoice in Figure 11.1 are:

1. Find each amount by multiplying the quantity by the unit price.
2. Add to find the subtotal.
3. Calculate the 2% discount—paid within 10 days.
4. Subtract to find the subtotal.
5. Calculate the amount of a 4% sales tax.
6. Add the tax to find the invoice total. Study the invoice and check each amount by carrying out the necessary calculations.

Customer:

Invoice
Number: 15490

PC Computer Shop

14095 Memory Drive

Computer City, USA 00495

CUSTOMER ORDER NO.	SALESMAN	TERMS	INVOICE PAID IN:	F.O.B.	DATE
A-10369	Justin	2/10, N/30	6 Days	—	3/25

ITEM	QUANTITY	DESCRIPTION	UNIT PRICE		AMOUNT	
0306	12	Memory chips	2	15	25	80
0315	6	RS-232 port connectors	7	40	44	40
0317	24	Multifunction board chips	5	10	122	40
		Subtotal			192	60
		discount			3	85
		Subtotal			188	75
		4% sales tax			7	55
		Invoice total			196	30

Figure 11.1. Sample invoice

EXERCISE 3: COMPLETING AN INVOICE

▶ Calculate the sales tax for each amount and percent.

1. $70 at 5% _____ 2. $460 at 7% _____
3. $102 at 8% _____ 4. $56.90 at 4% _____
5. $204.38 at 5% _____ 6. $874.30 at 5.5% _____
7. $89.73 at 6.5% _____ 8. $120.40 at 10% _____

▶ **9.** Complete the invoice in Figure 11.2:
1. Find each amount by multiplying the quantity by the unit price.
2. Add to find the subtotal.
3. Calculate the discount if the invoice is paid in 7 days.
4. Subtract to find the subtotal.
5. Calculate the amount of sales tax.
6. Add the tax to find the invoice total.

Customer:						Invoice Number: 15491	

Computer Service Co.

14 West Drive

Service City, USA   01222

CUSTOMER ORDER NO.	SALESMAN	TERMS	INVOICE PAID IN:	F.O.B.	DATE
B-20144	Jason	2/10, N/30	30 Days	—	3/26

ITEM	QUANTITY	DESCRIPTION	UNIT PRICE		AMOUNT	
1201	25	#10 Bolts	3	40		
1490	40	Fasteners	2	90		
1678	100	Port covers	6	00		
2347	67	Washers		49		
0055	115	Brackets	4	08		
0002	75	Bracket fasteners		67		
1237	10	Chip sockets	1	29		
		Subtotal				
		discount				
		Subtotal				
		4% Sales tax				
		Invoice total				

Figure 11.2. Practice invoice

Lesson 11
TOUCH DRILL FOR SPEED DEVELOPMENT

▶ Record the total number of minutes and seconds it takes to complete these exercises on the line provided. Calculate each sum.

1.	963	2.	787	3.	735	4.	195
	696		987		353		919
	936		797		357		591
	363		879		757		191

5.	78,454	6.	20,356	7.	12,450	8.	90,807
	78,054		23,065		40,502		70,809
	50,478		56,302		54,102		89,780
	78,405		36,520		12,204		70,990

▶ Subtract.

9.	70,361	10.	57,802	11.	89,808	12.	45,407
	−14,029		−19,890		−70,212		−81,713

13.	676,343	14.	673,080	15.	123,987	16.	654,456
	−121,909		−367,701		−357,951		−987,789

▶ Divide. Set your decimal selector at 0.

17. $24,860 \div 81$ 18. $16,480 \div 20$

19. $561,000 \div 300$ 20. $709,217 \div 465$

21. $978,351 \div 376$ 22. $6,891,008 \div 405$

▶ Find the sum for each problem below. Set your decimal selector at A. Remember that each entry must be a two-place decimal.

23.	609.00	24.	385.00	25.	34.66	26.	13.29
	127.04		190.33		908.77		874.00
	67.90		507.11		70.19		109.06
	12.85		120.93		148.28		198.37

27.	908.00	28.	908.00	29.	982.51	30.	176.00
	142.76		142.48		895.00		45.00
	809.75		78.09		109.20		109.00
	12.34		100.00		74.00		571.00

1. _____
2. _____
3. _____
4. _____
5. _____
6. _____
7. _____
8. _____
9. _____
10. _____
11. _____
12. _____
13. _____
14. _____
15. _____
16. _____
17. _____
18. _____
19. _____
20. _____
21. _____
22. _____
23. _____
24. _____
25. _____
26. _____
27. _____
28. _____
29. _____
30. _____

Name _____

Lesson 11
APPLY YOUR SKILLS

▶ Find the discount and total to be paid for each of the following:

	Amount	Terms	When Paid	Discount	Total
1.	$1,000	2/15	11 days	_____	_____
2.	$750.00	3/10	8 days	_____	_____
3.	$475.90	3/10, 2/20	15 days	_____	_____
4.	$509.35	3/10, 2/30	2 days	_____	_____
5.	$5,680.27	2/10, N/30	27 days	_____	_____

6. Complete the amounts for each item on the invoice (Figure 11.3). Find the subtotal, discount, second subtotal, sales tax, and invoice total.

Customer:

Invoice Number: 15492

Toyland, USA

720 Shopping Center Drive

Toy City, USA   01133

CUSTOMER ORDER NO.	SALESMAN	TERMS	INVOICE PAID IN:	F.O.B.	DATE
X-5022	Mary	3/10, 2/20, N/30	22 Days	—	4/1

ITEM	QUANTITY	DESCRIPTION	UNIT PRICE	AMOUNT
0679	34	Mix-match small cars #490	7 20	
0205	112	Teddy bear books #A21	98	
0102	96	Plastic army men #A-111	29	
0860	14	Dolls #624	4 77	
7211	25	Combination baseball sets	1 30	
0449	48	Card games	98	
0668	72	Rubber balls 1" diameter	70	
		Subtotal		
		discount		
		Subtotal		
		4% Sales tax		
		Invoice total		

Figure 11.3. Invoice for Apply Your Skills 1-6

▶ Find the discount and total to be paid for each of the following:

	Amount	Terms	When Paid	Discount	Total
7.	$2,500	2/10	11 days	_____	_____
8.	$805.00	3/15	12 days	_____	_____
9.	$572.15	2/15, 1/30	25 days	_____	_____
10.	$845.60	3/10, 2/30	16 days	_____	_____
11.	$7,950.00	2/10, N/30	10 days	_____	_____

12. Complete the amounts for each item on the invoice (Figure 11.4). Find the subtotal, discount, second subtotal, sales tax, and invoice total.

Invoice
Number: 15493

Auto Shop Inc.

1689 Engine Drive

Motor City, USA   01333

CUSTOMER ORDER NO.	SALESMAN	TERMS	INVOICE PAID IN:	F.O.B.	DATE
M-48321	Justin	2/10, N/30	9 Days	—	4/3

ITEM	QUANTITY	DESCRIPTION	UNIT PRICE		AMOUNT	
0043	80	Spark plug sets A465	2	29		
0542	112	Regular size wrenches		98		
0111	50	Auto shine polish	5	09		
7010	40	Clamps	1	07		
0009	120			98		
0784	70		1	39		
		Subtotal				
		discount				
		Subtotal				
		6% Sales tax				
		Invoice total				

Figure 11.4. Invoice for Apply Your Skills 7-12

Name_____

1. Find the total bill for a $40 item with an 8% sales tax.

   _____

2. Find the amount of a 6.5% discount on $450.80.

   _____

3. Calculate each of the following at terms of 2/10, N/30. The bill was paid in 9 days.

Subtotal	$786.59
Discount	_____
Subtotal	_____
5% Sales tax	_____
Invoice total	_____

4. Calculate each of the following at terms of 3/10, 1/30. The bill was paid in 19 days.

Subtotal	$15,607.00
Discount	_____
Subtotal	_____
5% Sales tax	_____
Invoice total	_____

5. If a sales tax is $5 on a bill of $200, what is the tax rate?

   _____

6. If a sales tax is $19.57 on a bill of $652.36, what is the tax rate?

   _____

Lesson 11
MASTERY CHECKPOINT

1. Find the total bill for a $95
   item with a 7% sales tax.

   _____

2. Find the amount of a 15%
   discount on an $8900.00 car.

   _____

3. Calculate each of the following
   at terms of 3/15, 1/30. The bill was
   paid in 2 days.

Subtotal	$1,483.29
Discount	_____
Subtotal	_____
5% Sales tax	_____
Invoice total	_____

4. Calculate each of the following
   at terms of 2/10, N/30. The bill was
   paid in 9 days.

Subtotal	$40,678.25
Discount	_____
Subtotal	_____
4.5% Sales tax	_____
Invoice total	_____

5. If a sales tax is $25.60 on a bill
   of $731.43, what is the tax rate?

   _____

6. If a sales tax is $50.25 on a bill of
   $2,010, what is the tax rate?

   _____

Name _____

LESSON **12**

MULTIPLE DISCOUNTS

OBJECTIVES

After completing this lesson you will be able to:

- Calculate discount amount, discount rate, and net cost.
- Calculate multiple discounts.
- Use the complementary method.

WORKING WITH PERCENTS

The triangle model for working with percents is shown again in Figure 12.1. Recall that if the rate and base are known, you find the amount by multiplying. If you know the amount and base or the amount and rate, you divide. The amount is on top in the triangle, so you divide it by rate or base.

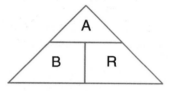

Figure 12.1. Triangle model for working with percents

DEMONSTRATION EXAMPLE

A TV set with a selling price of $560 is sold, after discount, for $476. Find the discount rate.

First, find the discount amount: 560 − 476 = 84.
You now know that the discount amount is $84.
To find the rate you must answer: 84 is what percent of 560?
To find the discount rate, divide: R = A/B = 84/560

Keystrokes:	84	÷	560	%
Display:	84	84	560	15

The discount rate is 15%.

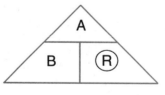

Figure 12.2. Triangle model for finding the rate

COMPLEMENTARY PERCENT

If a 20% discount is given on an item costing $960, we find that amount by multiplying:

Amount = Base x Rate

960 x 20% = $192

The selling price after the discount is found by subtracting the discount amount from the base selling price: $960 – $192 = $768. Since $768 is the amount after taking off a 20% discount, it is equal to 80% of the base. 80% is called the complementary percent. In general, you can find the complementary percent by subtracting a given percent from 100. Figure 12.3 represents $960.

20% of $960 = $192

80% of $960 = $768

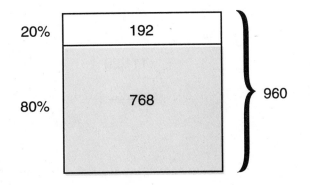

Figure 12.3. Determining complementary percent

DEMONSTRATION EXAMPLE

A 15% discount gives a net price of $178.50. Find the list price.

The net price is the amount after the discount has been subtracted.

We use the complementary discount: 100 – 15 = 85.

Therefore, $178.50 is 85% of what number?

We are looking for the base.

Base = 178.50 ÷ 85% = 210

The list price was $210.

EXERCISE 1: DETERMINING PRICES AND DISCOUNTS

▶ In each of the following, find the missing amounts or percents.

	List Price	Discount Rate	Discount Amount	Net Price
1.	1,350	_____ %	81	_____
2.	897	_____ %	_____	801.50
3.	1,551	_____ %	96.70	_____
4.	_____	12 %	_____	657.25
5.	2,360	_____ %	_____	1,998.40
6.	995	8 %	_____	_____
7.	1,675	3 1/2 %	_____	_____
8.	4,168	3 1/3 %	_____	_____
9.	2,780	_____ %	111.20	_____
10.	_____	13 %	_____	3,780

MULTIPLE DISCOUNTS

An item might sometimes be discounted more than once for certain customers. For example, a manufacturer might offer the following: (1) a 20% discount as an incentive to sell an older model; (2) a 20% trade discount to retailers; (3) a 5% cash purchase discount. Each successive discount is taken on the new net price.

The memory functions work a little differently on different calculators. Be sure to find out just how the memory works on your calculator. To retain a net price in memory, it is necessary, on some calculators, to work with percents as decimals.

DEMONSTRATION EXAMPLE 1

Find the multiple discounts and net prices on an item listed at $249, with discounts of 20%, 20%, and 5%.

List Price: $249
1st Discount: 20%
2nd Discount: 20%
3rd Discount: 5%
1st Discount

Discount amount	= List price x Discount rate
	= 249 x .20
	= 49.80
Net price	= List price – Discount amount
	= 249.00 – 49.80
	= 199.20

2nd Discount

Discount amount	= Net price after 1st discount x Discount rate
	= 199.20 x .20
	= 39.84
Net price	= Net price after 1st discount – Discount amount
	= 199.20 – 39.84
	= 159.36

3rd Discount

Discount amount	= Net price after 2nd discount x Discount rate
	= 159.36 x .05
	= 7.97
Net price	= Net price after 2nd discount – Discount amount
	= 159.36 – 7.97
	= 151.39

DEMONSTRATION EXAMPLE 2

Find the net price on an item listed at $460 with discounts of 20%, 10%, and 5%. If we are not interested in the amount of the discounts, then we can use complementary percents to find the net price.

The complements are: 20% —> 80%; 10% —> 90%; 5% —> 95%

460 x 80% x 90% x 95% = $314.64

EXERCISE 2: FINDING MULTIPLE DISCOUNTS

▶ Work the multiple discount problems in the decimal mode with 5/4 rounding. Since you will be dealing with dollars and cents, set the decimal selector at 2. None of the discount rates includes fractional percents, so a setting of 2 is appropriate whether you enter the discount rate as a percent, using the percent key, or as a decimal. Find each discount amount and net price.

1. List price 265.80

First discount	5%	_____	Net price	_____
Second discount	10%	_____	Net price	_____
Third discount	15%	_____	Net price	_____

2. List price 379.00

First discount	7%	_____	Net price	_____
Second discount	10%	_____	Net price	_____
Third discount	12%	_____	Net price	_____

3. List price 599.70

First discount	10%	_____	Net price	_____
Second discount	12%	_____	Net price	_____
Third discount	14%	_____	Net price	_____

4. List price 688.22

First discount	5%	_____	Net price	_____
Second discount	12%	_____	Net price	_____
Third discount	15%	_____	Net price	_____

5. List price 719.43

First discount	5%	_____	Net price	_____
Second discount	10%	_____	Net price	_____
Third discount	20%	_____	Net price	_____

6. List price 888.59

First discount	10%	_____	Net price	_____
Second discount	29%	_____	Net price	_____
Third discount	25%	_____	Net price	_____

7. List price 1,001.25

First discount	10%	_____	Net price	_____
Second discount	10%	_____	Net price	_____
Third discount	10%	_____	Net price	_____

8. List price 1,195.69

First discount	7% _____	Net price _____
Second discount	7% _____	Net price _____
Third discount	10% _____	Net price _____

9. List price 2,360.95

First discount	15% _____	Net price _____
Second discount	15% _____	Net price _____
Third discount	15% _____	Net price _____

10. List price 1,995.00

First discount	7% _____	Net price _____
Second discount	10% _____	Net price _____
Third discount	15% _____	Net price _____

11. List price 1,675.80

First discount	5% _____	Net price _____
Second discount	12% _____	Net price _____
Third discount	18% _____	Net price _____

▶ Use the complementary method to find each net cost.

12. List price 8,690.00
    First discount 10%; Second discount 15%; Third discount 20%;
        Net price _____.

13. List price 25,370.00
    First discount 10%; Second discount 12%; Third discount 12%;
        Net price _____.

14. List price 70.30
    First discount 5%; Second discount 5%; Third discount 10%;
        Net price _____.

15. List price 755.90
    First discount 7%; Second discount 7%; Third discount 10%;
        Net price _____.

16. List price 5,592.34
    First discount 10%; Second discount 10%; Third discount 10%;
        Net price _____.

Name _____

1. _____
2. _____
3. _____
4. _____
5. _____
6. _____
7. _____
8. _____
9. _____
10. _____
11. _____
12. _____
13. _____
14. _____
15. _____
16. _____
17. _____
18. _____
19. _____
20. _____
21. _____
22. _____
23. _____
24. _____
25. _____
26. _____
27. _____
28. _____
29. _____
30. _____

Lesson 12

TOUCH DRILL FOR SPEED DEVELOPMENT

▶ Record the total number of minutes and seconds it takes to complete this exercise on the line provided. Calculate each sum.

1.	2.	3.	4.
132	963	456	852
232	696	565	582
213	396	645	252
313	939	464	285

5.	6.	7.	8.
79,789	47,147	12,452	58,478
46,546	82,582	62,536	65,968
13,231	96,396	42,154	15,425
79,879	46,546	36,252	32,653

▶ Subtract.

9.	10.	11.	12.
90,657	50,102	89,021	86,571
−76,102	−49,008	−73,802	−50,003

13.	14.	15.	16.
673,190	897,060	683,091	382,901
−450,012	−916,372	−132,564	−564,645

▶ Divide. Set your decimal selector at 0.

17. $89,603 \div 65$ 18. $67,903 \div 76$

19. $708,942 \div 432$ 20. $978,606 \div 342$

21. $608,315 \div 168$ 22. $5,430,701 \div 200$

▶ Find the sum for each problem below. Set your decimal selector at A. Remember that each entry must be a two-place decimal.

23.	24.	25.	26.
745.00	756.08	90.87	45.07
317.09	165.50	305.76	132.67
41.80	143.66	40.10	576.00
30.00	756.00	432.00	698.01

27.	28.	29.	30.
978.34	756.32	815.39	632.00
560.00	780.00	173.93	98.00
143.78	31.78	285.46	612.00
99.00	709.30	90.00	786.00

Lesson 12
APPLY YOUR SKILLS

▶ Find the discount and total to be paid for each of the following.

	Amount	Terms	When Paid	Discount	Total
1.	$3,500	2/10	11 days	_____	_____
2.	$825.75	2/15	11 days	_____	_____
3.	$319.88	4/10, 2/20	8 days	_____	_____
4.	$709.53	3/10, N	7 days	_____	_____
5.	$5,000	2/10, 1/30	23 days	_____	_____

6. Complete the amounts for each item on the invoice. Find the subtotals, discounts, and invoice total.

Invoice
Number: 15494

Gifts Inc.

4782 E. Event Lane

Gift City, USA 00344

CUSTOMER ORDER NO.	SALESMAN	TERMS 20% Discount to Trade 3/10, 2/20, N/30	INVOICE PAID IN:	F.O.B.	DATE
69815	Jason		17 Days	—	4/3

ITEM	QUANTITY	DESCRIPTION	UNIT PRICE		AMOUNT	
4994	700	Candles		29		
2001	49	Candle holders	3	00		
0088	150	Calendars		50		
6733	60	Pen sets	1	55		
5987	65	Plaques	2	00		
0027	224	U.S.A. maps		19		
1266	80	Ashtrays		90		
		Subtotal				
		Trade discount				
		Subtotal				
		Purchase discount				
		Invoice total				

Figure 12.4. Invoice for Apply Your Skills 1-6

Name_____

▶ In each of the following, calculate the missing amounts.

	List price	Discount Rate	Discount Amount	Net Price
7.	$4,700	_____	_____	$4,324
8.	$5,500	7.5%	_____	_____
9.	_____	5%	$202	_____
10.	$3,108	_____	$466	_____
11.	$9,500	_____	_____	$1,900

12. Complete the amounts for each item on the invoice (Figure 12.5). Find the subtotals, discounts, and invoice total.

							Invoice
							Number: 15494

Corner Drug Store Inc.

2322 Avenue B

Anywhere, USA   00562

CUSTOMER ORDER NO.	SALESMAN	TERMS		INVOICE PAID IN:	F.O.B.	DATE
86-7201	John	25% Discount to Trade 3/15, 2/30, N/60		60 Days	–	4/4

ITEM	QUANTITY	DESCRIPTION	UNIT PRICE		AMOUNT	
0031	30	Lawn chairs	5	20		
0492	70	Iced tea glasses		75		
9802	120	#100 Film	1	50		
2377	90	Cassette tapes		80		
4621	170	Nail clipper sets		60		
0183	45	Sunglasses (Pairs)	2	09		
4707	24	Watchbands	1	75		
6200	48	Small ice chests		98		
		Subtotal				
		Trade discount				
		Subtotal				
		Purchase discount				
		Invoice total				

Figure 12.5. Invoice for Apply Your Skills 7-12

Lesson 12
CHECK YOUR PROGRESS

▶ Find the discount and total to be paid for each of the following.

	Amount	Terms	When Paid	Discount	Total
1.	$4,850.00	3/10	8 days	_____	_____
2.	$550.00	2/20	10 days	_____	_____
3.	$736.09	3/10, 2/20	12 days	_____	_____

▶ Calculate the missing amounts. Use the calculator's memory to avoid re-entering amounts.

4. List price 9,496.80

First discount	20%	_____	Net price	_____
Second discount	15%	_____	Net price	_____
Third discount	11%	_____	Net price	_____

5. List price 6,280.77

First discount	12%	_____	Net price	_____
Second discount	_____%	663.25	Net price	_____
Third discount	_____%	729.57	Net price	_____

Lesson 12
MASTERY CHECKPOINT

▶ In each of the following, calculate the missing amounts.

	List price	Discount Rate	Discount Amount	Net Price
1.	$8,000	15%	_____	_____
2.	$6,400	_____	_____	$5,760
3.	_____	17%	$137.53	_____

▶ Calculate the missing amounts. Use the calculator's memory to avoid re-entering amounts.

4. List price 10,350.00

First discount _____% _____ Net price 9,315

Second discount_____% _____ Net price 8,383

Third discount _____% _____ Net price 7,545

5. List price 24,955.28

First discount _____% _____ Net price 23,083

Second discount 15 % _____ Net price _____

Third discount _____% 3,029 Net price _____

MARKUP

OBJECTIVES

After completing this lesson, you will be able to:

- Calculate markup and markup rate based on percent of cost.
- Calculate markup and rate based on percent of selling price.

MARKUP BASED ON COST

Stores that sell to the general public are called retailers. To make a profit, the owner of a retail store must sell goods at an amount higher than the cost at which the item was purchased. This increase is called "markup." The percent rate of markup may be based on the cost of the item to the retailer or the retail price, that is, the amount the customer pays.

In the first part of this lesson, we consider markup based on cost. This kind of markup is called percent cost markup. In the second part, we consider markup based on selling price.

A retailer purchases a TV for $150 and marks it up 40% to arrive at a selling price. This means that she takes 40% of the $150 and then adds the percentage to the $150. Use your calculator to verify that 150 x 40% = 60. So the markup amount is $60. $150 + $60 = $210. The selling price is $210.

DEMONSTRATION EXAMPLE 1

A retailer purchases sweaters for $18 each and marks them up 45%. Find the amount of the markup.

Cost	x	Markup rate	=	Markup
18	x	45%	=	8.1

The amount of the markup is $8.10

EXERCISE 1: DETERMINING THE MARKUP

▶ Find the markup for each of the following.

	Cost	Markup Rate	Markup
1.	$50.00	15%	_____
2.	$245.00	25%	_____
3.	$578.00	33%	_____
4.	$439.80	30%	_____
5.	$890.10	42%	_____
6.	$900.68	37%	_____
7.	$456.75	41%	_____
8.	$789.02	40%	_____

DEMONSTRATION EXAMPLE 2

A store owner purchases an item for $225 and uses a 40% markup to set the selling price. Find the selling price.

Cost	x	Markup rate	=	Markup
225	x	40%	=	90

Cost	+	Markup	=	Selling price
225	+	90	=	315

On some business calculators, only four entries are needed:

Entry:	225	x	40%	+
Display:	225	225	90.00	315.00

EXERCISE 2: DETERMINING THE SELLING PRICE

▶ Find the markup and selling price for each of the following.

	Cost	Markup Rate	Markup	Selling Price
1.	$1,208.00	45%	_____	_____
2.	$3,290.50	39%	_____	_____
3.	$2,895.60	35%	_____	_____
4.	$4,560.86	40%	_____	_____
5.	$3,800.00	44%	_____	_____
6.	$4,801.20	38%	_____	_____
7.	$7,890.30	40%	_____	_____

We have been determining a selling price by adding the amount of markup to the original cost. Another way to find the selling price is to first add the markup rate to 100% and then multiply by the cost.

DEMONSTRATION EXAMPLE 3

A store owner purchases a lawn mower for $300 and marks it up 35%.

 What is the selling price?

 $300 is 100% of the cost.

 100% + 35% is the selling price as a percent of the cost.

 $300 x 135% = $405.

 The selling price is $405.

EXERCISE 3: USING THE MARKUP RATE

▶ Find the selling price for each of the following.

	Cost	Markup Rate	Selling Price
1.	$45	50%	_____
2.	$78	42%	_____
3.	$480	45%	_____
4.	$690	35%	_____
5.	$220.50	28%	_____

When you know the cost and the markup amount, you can find the markup rate by using the same method used to find a percent when the amount and base are known.

A markup of $50 is added to an item costing the store owner $160. We divide to find the rate of markup. $50 \div 160 = 0.3125$ or 31.25%.

DEMONSTRATION EXAMPLE 4

The cost of an item to a retailer is $510. The retailer then puts a selling price of $688.50 on the item. Find the markup and the percent rate of markup.

Step 1. To find markup, subtract cost from selling price.

Selling Price	–	Cost	=	Markup
688.50	–	510	=	178.50

Enter: 688.5 $\boxed{+}$ 510 $\boxed{-}$

Display: 688.5   688.5 510   178.5

Step 2. To find rate, divide markup by cost.

Enter: 178.50 $\boxed{\div}$ 510 $\boxed{\%}$

Display: 178.50   178.50 510   35.00

The two steps above may be combined as follows. If the numbers are large, this saves keystrokes by entering the cost only once.

Enter: 688.5 $\boxed{+}$ 510 $\boxed{M+}$ $\boxed{-}$ $\boxed{\div}$ $\boxed{RM}$ $\boxed{\%}$

Display: 688.5   688.5   510   510   178.5   178.5   510   35

Name _____

EXERCISE 4: FINDING THE MARKUP RATE

▶ Find the markup and percent cost markup. Set the decimal selector at 2. Use the % key.

	Cost	Retail	Markup	Percent
1.	$46.28	$62.84	$_____	$_____
2.	$59.45	$78.60	$_____	$_____
3.	$75.43	$94.25	$_____	$_____
4.	$86.15	$98.79	$_____	$_____
5.	$91.37	$98.59	$_____	$_____
6.	$127.93	$149.95	$_____	$_____
7.	$117.82	$215.39	$_____	$_____
8.	$164.27	$325.17	$_____	$_____
9.	$318.72	$449.88	$_____	$_____
10.	$681.34	$945.61	$_____	$_____

MARKUP BASED ON SELLING PRICE

Markup is sometimes calculated on the basis of the selling price, which is also the retail price. For example, if an item is selling for $400 and has been marked up an amount of $120, then you can find the markup rate using the percent method: 120 ÷ 400 = 30%

$$\text{Retail markup rate (\%)} = \text{Markup} \div \text{Retail price}$$

DEMONSTRATION EXAMPLE

Find the retail markup rate on an item that costs $267.50 and has a retail price of $355.78

Step 1. Find the markup by subtracting cost from selling price.

Retail Price	–	Cost	=	Markup
355.78	–	267.50	=	88.28

Step 2. Find the rate by dividing markup by retail price.

Markup	÷	Retail price	=	Markup rate		
88.28	÷	355.78	=	0.248	=	24.8%

Using memory, we have the following keystrokes:

Enter: 355.78 M+ + 267.5 − ÷ RM %

Display: 355.78 355.78 355.78 267.5 88.28 88.28 355.78 24.8

EXERCISE 5: FINDING THE RETAIL MARKUP RATE

▶ Find each markup and percent retail markup.

	Cost	Retail	Markup	Percent
1.	$149.95	$169.95	$_____	_____
2.	$98.50	$129.95	$_____	_____
3.	$110.00	$189.45	$_____	_____
4.	$424.98	$529.35	$_____	_____
5.	$689.32	$949.00	$_____	_____
6.	$968.14	$1,387.33	$_____	_____
7.	$1,269.02	$1,899.00	$_____	_____
8.	$1,419.76	$1,520.56	$_____	_____
9.	$1,643.20	$1,782.28	$_____	_____
10.	$2,420.25	$2,850.60	$_____	_____

Lesson 13
APPLY YOUR SKILLS

▶ Find the markup and percent cost markup. Set the decimal selector at 2. Use the % key.

	Cost	Retail	Markup	Percent
1.	$1,025.65	$1,998.45	$_____	_____
2.	$1,495.38	$1,665.79	$_____	_____
3.	$1,680.00	$2,540.00	$_____	_____
4.	$3,476.29	$7,516.93	$_____	_____
5.	$10,490.00	$19,087.36	$_____	_____
6.	$23,665.73	$29,740.36	$_____	_____

▶ Find each markup and percent retail markup.

7.	$10,090.28	$11,995.00	$_____	_____
8.	$13,089.32	$15,775.69	$_____	_____
9.	$25,016.52	$36,554.29	$_____	_____
10.	$14,889.00	$16,449.00	$_____	_____
11.	$6,750.00	$7,898.50	$_____	_____
12.	$7,280.19	$5,395.22	$_____	_____

Name _____

Lesson 13
CHECK YOUR PROGRESS

▶ Calculate the missing amounts. Calculate markup percent based on cost.

	Cost	Retail Price	Markup	Markup Rate (%)
1.	$4,000	$5,000	_____	_____
2.	$6,600	_____	$ 2,640	_____
3.	$3,250	_____	_____	15%
4.	$384	$495	_____	_____
5.	$275.10	_____	_____	35%
6.	$2,350.60	$3,400	_____	_____
7.	$3,435.56	_____	$835.24	_____
8.	$1,926.24	_____	_____	28.5%
9.	_____	$635.26	$246.25	_____
10.	_____	$2,348.21	$911.25	_____

Lesson 13
MASTERY CHECKPOINT

▶ Complete the table. Calculate markup rate based on retail price.

	Cost	Retail Price	Markup	Markup Rate (%)
1.	$10,500	$12,000	_____	_____
2.	$890	_____	$200	_____
3.	_____	$15,500	_____	24%
4.	_____	$9,670	$2,400	_____
5.	$23,680	$27,990	_____	_____
6.	_____	$750.88	_____	35.5%
7.	$1,246.75	_____	$498.50	_____
8.	$2,506.20	$3,676.25	_____	_____
9.	$780.64	_____	$100.00	_____
10.	_____	$ 5,498.02	_____	41.4%

Name _____

REVENUE, EXPENSES, AND PROFIT BY DIVISION

OBJECTIVES

After completing this lesson, you will be able to:

- Calculate revenue, expenses, and profit by division.
- Calculate percents based on sales and profit.
- Create pie charts and bar graphs based on percents.
- Use bar graphs to solve problems.

PERCENT REVENUE

Large companies often engage in several different businesses in various parts of the country. The ABX Company is in the car rental and the furniture moving business. It has four geographic divisions. Each division deals in both businesses.

The table below shows annual revenue by division for the rental and moving businesses. The percent of revenue for each region is found by dividing the division's total revenue by the grand total, 5476:

$$\text{Regional percent} = \frac{\text{Division's total revenue}}{\text{Grand total}}$$

Revenue by Division (amounts in thousands)

	East	Midwest	West	South	Total	Average
Rev: Rental	532	691	437	906	2,566	641.5
Moving	912	1,406	215	377	2,910	727.5
Total Rev.	1,444	2,097	652	1,283	5,476	1,369
% Revenue	26.4%	38.3%	11.9%	23.4%		

The percent revenue for each division can be found by placing the total revenue (5,476) in memory (or using the constant function) and then dividing each division's revenue by the total revenue.

PIE CHARTS

A pie chart shows amounts as parts or sectors of a circle. Pie charts are usually used to illustrate percentages of a whole, such as expenditures for parts of a business.

The pie chart shows the revenues by division for the data in the table on page 162. Twenty-five percent would be one-fourth of the circle. Twelve percent is about one-eighth of the circle.

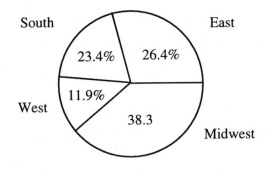

Figure 14.1.   Sample pie chart

EXERCISE 1: CALCULATING REVENUE, EXPENSES, PROFIT BY DIVISION

▶ The table below shows the 1993 revenues, expenses, and profits for the different businesses of the ABX company. It shows the financial information for four different divisions of the company.

Percent revenue (% Revenue) means a region's revenue as a percent of the total for the four regions.

Average means the average for the four regions: total divided by 4.

Profits are found by subtracting total expenses from total revenue. Percent profit is the division's profit as a percent of total profit. Complete the following table:

Revenue and Expenses by Division (amounts in thousands)

	East	Midwest	West	South	Total	Average
Rev: Rental	617	701	329	1,234	_____	_____
Moving	1,245	987	550	703	_____	_____
Total Rev.	_____	_____	_____	_____	_____	_____
% Revenue	_____	_____	_____	_____		
Exp: Salaries	826	739	460	237	_____	_____
Upkeep	321	299	203	561	_____	_____
Car Impr.	250	167	94	329	_____	_____
Total Exp.	_____	_____	_____	_____	_____	_____
Profit	_____	_____	_____	_____	_____	_____
% Profit	_____	_____	_____	_____		

▶ Use the percent figures to create pie charts for revenues and profits by division.

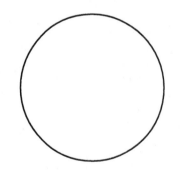

Figure 14.2. Revenues by division

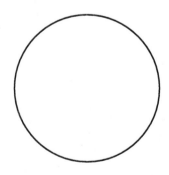

Figure 14.3. Profits by division

EXERCISE 2: CALCULATING REVENUE, EXPENSES, PROFIT BY QUARTER

▶ The same kind of table that shows revenue, expenses, and profit by division can be used to show the same categories for each of the four quarters of a year. Complete the following table.

% Revenue means the total revenue for the quarter as a percent of the total revenue for the year. Profit is found by subtracting total expenses from total revenue. Average means the average of the four quarters: the total for the four quarters divided by 4. Complete the following table:

Revenue and Expenses by Quarter (amounts in thousands)

	First	Second	Third	Fourth	Total	Average
Rev: Rental	437	578	751	563	_____	_____
Moving	987	621	1,207	825	_____	_____
Total Rev.	_____	_____	_____	_____	_____	_____
% Revenue	_____	_____	_____	_____		
Exp: Salaries	204	198	235	291	_____	_____
Upkeep	75	68	71	95	_____	_____
Car Impr.	221	201	198	220	_____	_____
Total Exp.	_____	_____	_____	_____	_____	_____
Profit	_____	_____	_____	_____	_____	_____
% Profit	_____	_____	_____	_____		

▶ Use the percent figures to create pie charts showing revenue and profit by quarter.

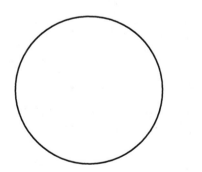

Figure 14.4. Revenue by quarter

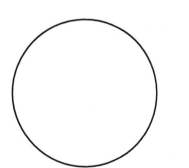

Figure 14.5. Profit by quarter

Name _____

BAR GRAPHS

A bar graph shows quantities according to the lengths of bars. A scale shows quantities such as amount of money or number of people. The length of the bars on the graph can be measured based on the scale. This kind of graph is often used to illustrate year-to-year amounts.

The graph shows revenues in hundreds of thousands for the Alpha Company since its founding.

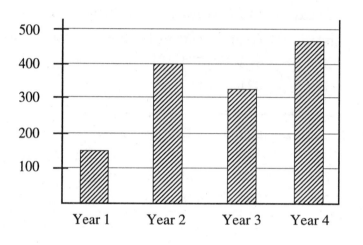

Figure 14.6. Bar graph 1

EXERCISE 3: WORKING WITH BAR GRAPHS

▶ Refer to Bar graph 1 (Figure 14.6) and answer the following questions:

1. What is the approximate revenue amount in Year 1? _____

2. Find the approximate increase from Year 1 to Year 2. _____

3. Find the approximate total revenue for the four years. _____

4. Find Year 1 revenue as an approximate percent of total revenue for the four years. _____

Sometimes a single bar can be used to show two amounts that combine to equal the total amount of the bar. Bar graph 2 below (Figure 14.7) shows numbers of workers for different years. The workers are divided into two general categories: farming and business/industry. These are distinguished on the graph by different patterns.

Workers in Monroe County (Amounts in thousands)

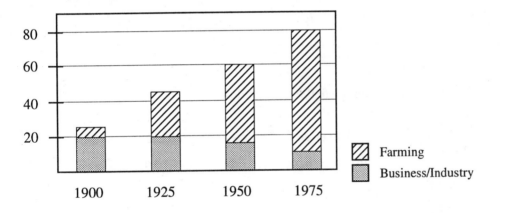

Figure 14.7.   Bar graph 2

▶ Find each answer as accurately as possible based on the graph in Figure 14.7.

5. How many farm workers were there in 1900? _____

6. What was the total number of workers in 1900? _____

7. How many workers were there in business/industry in 1900? _____

8. What was the increase in business/industry from 1900 to 1925? _____

9. What was the percentage of farm workers in relation to the total number of workers in 1925? _____

10. What was the pecentage of business/industry workers in relation to the total number of workers in 1975? _____

Name _____

Lesson 14
APPLY YOUR SKILLS

Bar graph 3 below (Figure 14.8) shows revenue and profit by quarter for a publishing company. The divisions are: B, books; M, magazines; N, newspapers. The full bars show revenue. The lower portion of each bar shows profit.

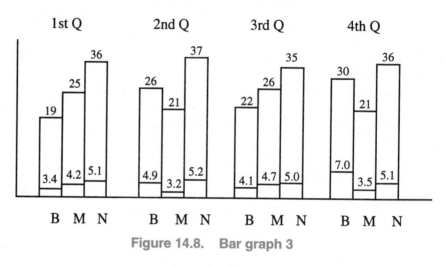

Figure 14.8. Bar graph 3

▶ Use the bar graph to complete the tables below.

Revenue by Quarter (amounts in thousands)

	First	Second	Third	Fourth	Total	Average
1. Rev: Books	_____	_____	_____	_____	_____	_____
2. Mag.	_____	_____	_____	_____	_____	_____
3. Newsp.	_____	_____	_____	_____	_____	_____
4. Total Rev.	_____	_____	_____	_____	_____	_____
5. % Revenue	_____	_____	_____	_____		

Profit by Quarter (amounts in thousands)

	First	Second	Third	Fourth	Total	Average
6. Profit: Books	_____	_____	_____	_____	_____	_____
7. Mag.	_____	_____	_____	_____	_____	_____
8. Newsp.	_____	_____	_____	_____	_____	_____
9. Total Profit	_____	_____	_____	_____	_____	_____
10. % Profit	_____	_____	_____	_____		

▶ Use pie chart 1 to find each answer. Total revenue for the company is $176,000.

1. Amount of revenue by division:

   A = _____ B = _____
   C = _____ D = _____

2. Find the profit by division based on the following percents of revenue by division. That is, percent profit = profit ÷ revenue.

   A (15.5%) _____ B (22.7%) _____
   C (28.1%) _____ D (8.5%) _____

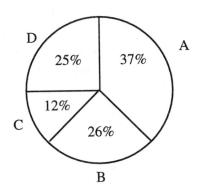

Figure 14.9. Pie chart 1

3. Partition the circle to form a graph showing profits by division.

Profits by Division

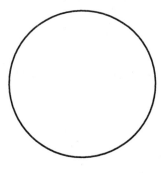

Figure 14.10   Pie chart 2

Name _____

Lesson 14
MASTERY CHECKPOINT

Bar graph 4 below (Figure 14.11) shows revenue by division by quarter. Amounts are in thousands.

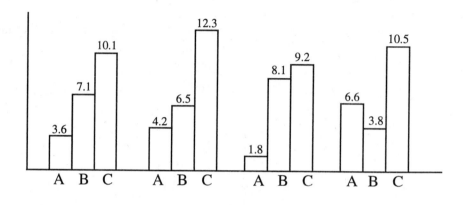

Figure 14.11.   Bar graph 4

▶ Use the graph to complete the table.

Revenue by Quarter (amounts in thousands)

		First	Second	Third	Fourth	Total	Average
Rev:	Div. A	_____	_____	_____	_____	_____	_____
	Div. B	_____	_____	_____	_____	_____	_____
	Div. C	_____	_____	_____	_____	_____	_____
Total Rev.		_____	_____	_____	_____	_____	_____
% Revenue		_____	_____	_____	_____		

PAYROLL

OBJECTIVES

After completing this lesson you will be able to:

- Calculate overtime rate and wages.
- Calculate taxes based on wages and tax rates.
- Calculate net pay based on wages and deductions.

CALCULATING PAYROLL

A payroll is a list of a company's employees and the wages due to each of them. The payroll includes gross earnings, any deductions, and net pay. Gross earnings means the wages before deductions—based on hourly work or on a salary.

Deductions can include federal, state, and local income tax, social security (listed as FICA for the Federal Insurance Contributions Act), medical and/or disability insurance, pension fund, and savings plans. Taxes to be withheld are required by law, but most other deductions are voluntary.

To calculate payroll, you must first determine gross earnings. Then you subtract deductions from gross earnings to find net pay. Net pay is often called "take-home pay."

Many jobs pay a certain hourly rate for the first 40 hours worked in a week and a higher overtime rate for any hours above 40. This overtime rate is generally 1.5 times the regular rate.

DEMONSTRATION EXAMPLE 1

Find the regular pay, the overtime pay, and the gross wages for a person who worked 46 hours in one week at a regular rate of $6.50 per hour and an overtime rate of 1.5 times the regular rate.

Regular pay: $40 \times 6.5 = 260$

Overtime rate: $6.5 \times 1.5 = 9.75$

Overtime pay: $6 \times 9.75 = 58.50$

Gross wages: $260 + 58.50 = 318.50$

Using memory these calculations are as follows:

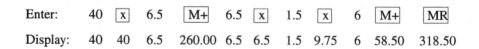

Enter:	40	☒	6.5	M+	6.5	☒	1.5	☒	6	M+	MR
Display:	40	40	6.5	260.00	6.5	6.5	1.5	9.75	6	58.50	318.50

EXERCISE 1: CALCULATING WAGES

1. Find the overtime rate for each at 1.5 times the regular rate.

2. At 40 hours for regular pay, find regular and overtime pay.

Regular Rate	Overtime Rate	Total Hours	Regular Pay	Overtime
$7.00	_____	47	_____	_____
$6.84	_____	38	_____	_____
$9.73	_____	52	_____	_____

▶ Calculate all the missing entries for the payroll summaries shown below. Use an overtime rate of 1.5 times the regular rate.

Total Gross Wages Summary

Employee Name	Hours	Rate/ Hour Regular Time	Total Over- time Hours	Over- time Rate/ Hour	Wages for Regular Hours	Wages for Over- time Hours	Total Wages
3. Berge, G.	45	7.50	____	____	____	____	____
4. Doe, J.	38	10.50	____	____	____	____	____
5. Ellis, M.	37	15.75	____	____	____	____	____
6. Jones, J.	52	21.80	____	____	____	____	____
Total	172				____	____	____

Total Gross Wages Summary

Employee Name	Hours	Rate/ Hour Regular Time	Total Over- time Hours	Over- time Rate/ Hour	Wages for Regular Hours	Wages for Over- time Hours	Total Wages
7. Donovan, B.	42	22.75	____	____	____	____	____
8. Roe, B.	43	18.60	____	____	____	____	____
9. Johnson, S.	35	16.25	____	____	____	____	____
10. McNeil, R.	51	15.50	____	____	____	____	____
Total	____				____	____	____

Name _____

DEDUCTIONS

Some deductions are based on percentages of gross wages. To calculate these amounts, you work with percents as you have in previous lessons. Federal tax is based on tax tables and varies according to the wages and number of dependents. Dependents are people who depend on someone else for financial support.

DEMONSTRATION EXAMPLE

The following deductions are based on the gross wages and percentages shown. Use your calculator to check each one.

Gross Wages	Federal Tax	Insurance	State Tax	FICA	Net Pay
		3.6%	4.5%	7.65%	
290	24.17	10.44	13.05	22.19	220.15

Using 290 as a constant, you can work the above calculations using the keystrokes shown. If your calculator uses the first number in multiplication as the constant, then you should subtract federal tax last as shown.

290   M+

X

3.6   %   M-   (Insurance)

4.5   %   M-   (State tax)

7.65   %   M-   (FICA)

24.17   M-   (Federal tax)

RM

EXERCISE 2: CALCULATING DEDUCTIONS AND NET PAY

▶ For each of the following, calculate each deduction and net pay.

	Name	Gross Wages	Federal Tax	Insurance 2.6%	State Tax 3.25%	FICA 7.65%	Net Pay
1.	Ashe	317	29.71	_____	_____	_____	_____
2.	Best	488.20	37.61	_____	_____	_____	_____
3.	Clark	506.14	42.08	_____	_____	_____	_____
4.	Dinzo	248.70	23.07	_____	_____	_____	_____
5.	Ernst	403.56	35.17	_____	_____	_____	_____
6.	Gold	311.84	25.90	_____	_____	_____	_____
7.	Holz	529.41	19.53	_____	_____	_____	_____
8.	Kelly	365.18	20.55	_____	_____	_____	_____
9.	Luis	498.37	26.59	_____	_____	_____	_____
10.	Mot	410.42	31.87	_____	_____	_____	_____

Name _____

1. _____
2. _____
3. _____
4. _____
5. _____
6. _____
7. _____
8. _____
9. _____
10. _____
11. _____
12. _____
13. _____
14. _____
15. _____
16. _____
17. _____
18. _____
19. _____
20. _____
21. _____
22. _____
23. _____
24. _____
25. _____
26. _____
27. _____
28. _____
29. _____
30. _____

Lesson 15

TOUCH DRILL FOR SPEED DEVELOPMENT

▶ Record the total number of minutes and seconds it takes to complete these exercises on the line provided. Calculate each sum.

1.	151	2.	858	3.	785	4.	486
	757		454		523		426
	959		252		475		716
	353		656		965		826

5.	40,506	6.	48,625	7.	18,353	8.	40,806
	70,809		79,135		38,185		10,203
	10,203		84,105		90,610		70,209
	60,804		60,503		72,825		60,302

▶ Subtract.

9.	71,029	10.	74,147	11.	80,634	12.	86,573
	−42,936		−58,285		−69,436		−34,383

13.	102,070	14.	704,030	15.	130,210	16.	620,320
	−305,080		−102,031		− 90,340		−569,031

▶ Multiply. Set your decimal selector at 0.

17. 298 x 721   18. 301 x 20
19. 231 x 12   20. 213 x 50
21. 867 x 31   22. 654 x 50

▶ Find the sum for each problem below. Set your decimal selector at A. Remember that each entry must be a two-place decimal.

23.	723.09	24.	120.30	25.	46.87	26.	57.53
	401.78		413.21		320.01		657.15
	60.09		910.20		21.35		156.53
	21.05		312.75		438.21		505.05

27.	764.23	28.	712.38	29.	419.80	30.	465.60
	980.12		731.38		729.30		79.89
	128.03		28.19		817.20		132.32
	19.27		172.38		17.28		506.40

Lesson 15
APPLY YOUR SKILLS

▶ Use a regular base of 40 hours and overtime at 1.5 times regular hourly pay to calculate the following total wages. Then use the total wages to calculate deductions and net pay. Calculate the total gross wage:

Total Gross Wages Summary

Employee Name	Total Hours	Rate/ Hour Regular Time	Total Over- time Hours	Over- time Rate/ Hour	Wages for Regular Hours	Wages for Over- time Hours	Total Wages
A. Grindy, L.	42	24.25	_____	_____	_____	_____	_____
B. Vacario, V.	46	14.50	_____	_____	_____	_____	_____
C. Waters, B.	49	19.60	_____	_____	_____	_____	_____
D. Kumler, R.	39	21.80	_____	_____	_____	_____	_____
E. Weinstein, G.	40	23.80	_____	_____	_____	_____	_____
Total	_____				_____	_____	_____

▶ Calculate the deductions and net pay for the following. Use the gross wages you calculated in exercise 1.

Deductions and Net Pay Summary

Employee Name	Gross Wages	Federal Income Taxes	Insurance 5.5%	State Tax 6.1%	Retire- ment 6%	FICA 7.1%	Net Pay
A. Grindy, L.		85.20	_____	_____	_____	_____	_____
B. Vacario, V.		57.46	_____	_____	_____	_____	_____
C. Waters, B.		61.44	_____	_____	_____	_____	_____
D. Kumler, R.		78.35	_____	_____	_____	_____	_____
E. Weinstein, G.		81.50	_____	_____	_____	_____	_____
Total	_____	_____	_____	_____	_____	_____	_____

Name _____

Lesson 15
CHECK YOUR PROGRESS

▶ Calculate the total wages for each of the following:

Total Gross Wages Summary

Employee Name	Total Hours	Rate/ Hour Regular Time	Total Over- time Hours	Over- time Rate/ Hour	Wages for Regular Hours	Wages for Over- time Hours	Total Wages
K. Hatch	48	14.25	____	____	____	____	____
A. Irace	39	18.75	____	____	____	____	____
P. Krom	47	19.60	____	____	____	____	____
C. Mendez	40	15.20	____	____	____	____	____
N. Nole	40	8.50	____	____	____	____	____
Total	____	____	____	____	____	____	____

Lesson 15
MASTERY CHECKPOINT

▶ Calculate the deductions and net pay for each of the following employees. Use the gross wages you calculated in Check Your Progress.

Deductions and Net Pay Summary

Employee Name	Gross Wages	Federal Income Taxes	Insurance 5.5%	State Tax 6.1%	Retire-ment 6%	FICA 7.1%	Net Pay
K. Hatch	_____	64.28	_____	_____	_____	_____	_____
A. Irace	_____	56.09	_____	_____	_____	_____	_____
P. Krom	_____	72.13	_____	_____	_____	_____	_____
C. Mendez	_____	48.72	_____	_____	_____	_____	_____
N. Nole	_____	31.65	_____	_____	_____	_____	_____
Total	_____	_____	_____	_____	_____	_____	_____

Name _____

LESSON **16**

PERCENT OF INCREASE OR DECREASE AND PRORATING

OBJECTIVES

After completing this lesson, you will be able to:

- Calculate percent of increase or decrease.
- Calculate amount of increase or decrease based on percent.
- Allocate expenses according to sales distribution.

SALES FIGURES

Business managers and accountants watch sales closely because sales figures indicate the growth or decline of a company. An increase or decrease in sales is usually measured as a percent. On your calculator, a negative amount is indicated by a negative sign *after* the number. On printing calculators, negative amounts are often printed in red. In financial documents, negative amounts and negative percents are usually placed in parentheses. People reading the statements know that this means the amount is negative. For this lesson, set your decimal selector at 2.

DEMONSTRATION EXAMPLE 1

A company had sales of $567,300 last year and sales of $642,200 this year. Find the amount of increase or decrease in sales and the percent of increase or decrease based on last year's sales volume.

This year's sales	–	Last year's sales	=	Amt. increase or decrease
642,200	–	567,300	=	74,900 (increase)

To find the percent of increase, divide the increase by last year's sales amount.

Keystrokes	74,900	÷		567,300	%
Display	74,900	74,900		567,300	13.20

DEMONSTRATION EXAMPLE 2

Company ADR had sales of $342,800 last year and sales of $287,500 this year. Find the amount of the increase or decrease and the percent of increase or decrease based on last year's sales.

This year's sales	–	Last year's sales	=	Amt. increase or decrease
287,500	–	342,800	=	(55,300)

To find the percent of decrease, divide the decrease by last year's sales amount:

Keystrokes	55,300	–		÷	342,800	%
Display	55,300	55,300	55,300	342,800		16.13–

EXERCISE 1: CALCULATING PERCENT INCREASES AND DECREASES

▶ Calculate the amount and percent of increase or decrease. Indicate a decrease by enclosing the figures in parentheses.

	This Year	Last Year	Increase/ Decrease	Percent
1.	$1,690.00	$2,380.00	$_____	_____%
2.	$3,150.00	$2,990.36	$_____	_____%
3.	$3,862.00	$4,650.25	$_____	_____%
4.	$6,895.40	$5,906.00	$_____	_____%
5.	$8,535.06	$9,176.61	$_____	_____%
6.	$12,334.45	$10,998.47	$_____	_____%
7.	$17,452.83	$19,246.35	$_____	_____%
8.	$22,350.35	$21,987.66	$_____	_____%
9.	$88,461.19	$87,968.23	$_____	_____%
10.	$49,540.00	$48,539.75	$_____	_____%
11.	$62,170.49	$64,480.00	$_____	_____%
12.	$71,380.00	$91,572.30	$_____	_____%
13.	$168,291.35	$159,360.00	$_____	_____%
14.	$129,303.66	$141,060.35	$_____	_____%
15.	$155,110.00	$149,209.41	$_____	_____%
16.	$69,850.00	$46,800.75	$_____	_____%

▶ You will be starting with different data in problems 17–25. Work each of these problems in as few steps as possible.

	This Year	Last Year	Increase/ Decrease	Percent
17.	$34,775.00	$_____	$8,975.00	_____%
18.	$_____	$18,065.35	$10,350.00	_____%
19.	$25,380.45	$_____	$1,650.00	_____%
20.	$_____	$_____	$10,965.20	28.46%
21.	$14,500.00	$16,100.00	$_____	_____%
22.	$72,652.00	$_____	$(9,127.50)	_____%
23.	$52,784.60	$_____	$_____	(12.4%)
24.	$19,691.00	$_____	$1,201.00	_____%
25.	$_____	$_____	$(9,650.00)	(9.3%)

Percent distribution of sales or expenses is similar to the distributions in Lesson 14. First you must find the total amount of sales. Then you can find percents by dividing the sales of each department by the total. The following formula will give you percent sales for a department.

Department sales   "   Total sales   =   %

For speed and accuracy in calculating, after you find the total, you may enter it as a constant and use this to find the different percents.

Name _____

EXERCISE 2: CALCULATING TOTAL SALES AND PERCENT

▶ Calculate the total sales and percent by division for each problem. Calculate percents as two-place decimals. The total of percents should be very close to 100. It may be a little above or below 100 because of rounding.

1.

Department	Sales for Quarter	Percent of Total
A	$ 10,350	_____
B	19,808	_____
C	26,225	_____
D	46,030	_____
E	89,450	_____
F	120,300	_____
G	20,950	_____
TOTAL	$_____	_____

2.

Department	Sales for Quarter	Percent of Total
A	$ 135,000	_____
B	10,280	_____
C	46,350	_____
D	20,080	_____
E	98,360	_____
F	110,200	_____
G	67,020	_____
H	19,670	_____
I	46,086	_____
TOTAL	$_____	_____

3.

Department	Sales for Quarter	Percent of Total
A	$ 498	_____
B	69,225	_____
C	3,627	_____
D	10,980	_____
E	1,450	_____
F	9,275	_____
G	7,080	_____
H	14,260	_____
I	24,388	_____
J	36,490	_____
TOTAL	$_____	_____

PRORATING SALES AND EXPENSES

▶ Prorating means dividing a total quantity into parts according to percentages or ratios. Suppose, for example, three people own the following percentage of a company: Jones, 50%; Martinez, 30%; Parks, 20%. The profits of the company would then be prorated according to these percents.

DEMONSTRATION EXAMPLE

JMP Company is owned in the following percents: Jones, 50%; Martinez, 30%; Parks, 20%. How much should each of the owners receive if total profits are $80,000? To find the amounts, $80,000 must be prorated:

Jones	80,000 x 50 % = 40,000	Jones receives $40,000
Martinez	80,000 x 30 % = 24,000	Martinez receives $24,000
Parks	80,000 x 20 % = 16,000	Parks receives $16,000

EXERCISE 3: PRORATING

▶ Prorate the total according to the given percents.

1. Valu Company has four owners. How much of the total profits will each receive according to the percent of ownership?

Owner	Percent	Amount of Profits
Baker	40%	_____
Golden	22%	_____
Clancy	9%	_____
Wu	29%	_____
Total	_____	$65,400

2. Charges for utilities are prorated by department according to the given percents. Find the amount to be paid by each department in each category. Find answers to the nearest dollar.

Department	Percent	Heat	Electricity	Maintenance
A	36%	_____	_____	_____
B	28%	_____	_____	_____
C	17%	_____	_____	_____
D	12%	_____	_____	_____
E	7%	_____	_____	_____
Total	_____	$4,378	$3,860	$7,271

Lesson 16
APPLY YOUR SKILLS

Some companies assign expenses to departments according to sales distribution. The easiest way to calculate such prorations is to form a fraction so that departmental sales as a portion of total sales are multiplied by the total expenses. This method allocates an amount of expenses that is proportional to the department's sales.

DEMONSTRATION EXAMPLE

(Decimal is set on 2 and 5/4 rounding.)

Total expenses: $2,135

Department	Sales	Share of Expenses
A	$16,487	$ 531.38
B	10,250	330.36
C	13,490	434.79
D	17,235	555.49
E	8,780	282.98
Total	$66,242	$ 2,135.00

Total sales = Sum of sales for all departments
= 16,487 + 10,250 + 13,490 + 17,235 + 8,780
= 66,242

$$\text{Share of expenses} = \frac{\text{Department sales x Total expenses}}{\text{Total sales}}$$

$$= \frac{16,487 \times 2,135}{66,242}$$

$$= 531.38$$

▶ Use the decimal mode and 5/4 rounding. Set the decimal at 4 for greater accuracy, but round answers to two decimal places (dollars and cents).

1. Total expenses: $3,490

Department	Sales	Share of Expenses
A	$9,860	$_____
B	15,340	_____
C	23,100	_____
D	13,725	_____
E	11,490	_____
F	4,180	_____
Total	$_____	$_____

Name _____

2. Total expenses: $19,360

Department	Sales	Share of Expenses
A	$10,350	$_____
B	19,808	_____
C	26,225	_____
D	46,030	_____
E	89,450	_____
F	120,300	_____
G	20,950	_____
Total	$_____	$_____

3. Total expenses: $23,490

Department	Sales	Share of Expenses
A	$135,000	$_____
B	10,280	_____
C	46,350	_____
D	20,080	_____
E	98,360	_____
F	110,200	_____
G	67,020	_____
H	19,670	_____
Total	$_____	$_____

4. Total expenses: $7,650

Department	Sales	Share of Expenses
A	$69,225	$_____
B	498	_____
C	3,627	_____
D	10,980	_____
E	1,450	_____
F	9,275	_____
G	7,080	_____
H	14,260	_____
Total	$_____	$_____

Lesson 16
CHECK YOUR PROGRESS

▶ Calculate the amount and percent of increase or decrease. Indicate a decrease by enclosing the amounts in parentheses.

	This Year	Last Year	Increase/ (Decrease)	% Increase/ (Decrease)
1.	$12,300	$11,100	_____	_____
2.	$15,600	$17,600	_____	_____
3.	$19,460	_____	$2,190	_____
4.	$50,210	_____	($3,260)	_____
5.	_____	$23,740	$4,290	_____

▶ Allocate expenses of $7,620 proportionately to sales of the departments.

	Department	Sales	Expenses
6.	A	$7,420	_____
7.	B	2,140	_____
8.	C	4,980	_____
9.	D	10,410	_____
10.	E	920	_____
11.	Total	_____	_____

Name _____

Lesson 16
MASTERY CHECKPOINT

▶ Calculate the amount and percent of increase or decrease. Indicate a decrease by enclosing the figures in parentheses.

	This Year	Last Year	Increase/ (Decrease)	% Increase/ (Decrease)
1.	$41,000	$45,000	_____	_____
2.	$31,250	$28,910	_____	_____
3.	$37,600	_____	($4,590)	_____
4.	$98,020	_____	$ 9,870	_____
5.	_____	$23,740	_____	(15.4%)

▶ Allocate expenses of $67,500 proportionately to sales of the departments. Calculate the percent of expenses allocated to each department.

	Department	Sales	% Expenses	Expenses
6.	A	$65,030	_____	_____
7.	B	8,760	_____	_____
8.	C	28,400	_____	_____
9.	D	17,300	_____	_____
10.	E	6,350	_____	_____
11.	Total	_____	_____	_____

LESSON **17**

SALES QUOTAS

OBJECTIVES

After completing this lesson, you will be able to:

- Calculate dollar and percent differences between actual sales and sales quotas.
- Calculate dollar and percent differences between budgeted and actual sales and between actual and projected sales.

WORKING WITH QUOTAS

As an aid to planning, companies often set sales goals called "sales quotas" for the amount of sales they expect. Departments and individual salespersons have quotas, and their actual sales are later compared with the quotas. The following example shows sales by department, quotas, the differences between actual sales and sales quotas, and the percent differences.

DEMONSTRATION EXAMPLE

Department	Sales	Quota	Dollar Difference	Percent Over/Under Quota
A	$16,487	$15,450	$1,037	6.71
B	10,250	13,300	(3,050)	(22.93)
C	13,490	15,000	(1,510)	(10.07)
D	17,235	16,780	455	2.71
E	8,780	9,000	(220)	(2.44)
Total	$66,242	$69,530	($3,288)	(4.73)

$$\text{Dollar difference} = \text{Sales} - \text{Quota}$$
$$= 16,487 - 15,450$$
$$= 1,037$$

$$\text{Percent over/under quota} = \text{Dollar difference} \div \text{Quota}$$
$$= 1,037 \div 15,450$$
$$= 6.71\%$$

Negative dollar differences are enclosed in parentheses in the table. Department B, for example, was under quota.

Note the following vocabulary. A *sales quota* is the amount of sales expected. A sales goal is what a department is expected to meet or surpass. The *dollar difference* is the difference between actual sales for a given time period and the quota for that period, expressed in dollars. In other words, it is the dollar amount by which a department is over or under quota. *Percent over/under quota* means the amount by which a department is over or under quota, expressed as a percent of the quota.

EXERCISE 1: CALCULATING SALES GOALS

▶ Use the decimal mode and 5/4 rounding. Set the decimal at 2 and use the percent key. When a department is under quota, indicate the negative dollar difference and percent by enclosing the difference in parentheses, as in the example.

▶ Calculate the following:

Department	Sales	Quota	Dollar Difference	Percent Over/Under Quota
A	$ 9,860	$ 9,500	$_____	_____
B	15,340	15,800	_____	_____
C	23,100	24,500	_____	_____
D	13,725	12,500	_____	_____
E	4,180	2,775	_____	_____
Total	$_____	$_____	$_____	_____

▶ Calculate the following:

Department	Sales	Quota	Dollar Difference	Percent Over/Under Quota
A	$ 10,350	$ 9,675	$_____	_____
B	19,808	21,300	_____	_____
C	26,225	27,900	_____	_____
D	46,030	45,000	_____	_____
E	89,450	70,000	_____	_____
F	120,300	136,985	_____	_____
G	20,950	27,500	_____	_____
Total	$_____	$_____	$_____	_____

Name _____

Calculate the following:

Department	Sales	Quota	Dollar Difference	Percent Over/Under Quota
A	$135,000	$139,000	$_____	_____
B	10,280	15,000	_____	_____
C	46,350	49,500	_____	_____
D	20,080	16,750	_____	_____
E	98,360	105,225	_____	_____
F	110,200	100,000	_____	_____
G	67,020	70,900	_____	_____
H	19,670	21,000	_____	_____
I	46,086	46,000	_____	_____
Total	$_____	$_____	$_____	_____

Calculate the following:

Department	Sales	Quota	Dollar Difference	Percent Over/Under Quota
A	$ 498	$ 450	$_____	_____
B	69,225	70,000	_____	_____
C	3,627	3,000	_____	_____
D	10,980	12,225	_____	_____
E	1,450	1,500	_____	_____
F	9,275	10,000	_____	_____
G	7,080	6,500	_____	_____
H	14,260	15,800	_____	_____
I	24,388	26,390	_____	_____
J	36,490	35,500	_____	_____
Total	$_____	$_____	$_____	_____

BUDGET ANALYSIS

A budgeted amount is like a quota. A quota is usually applied to sales goals. But a budgeted amount may be applied to sales, expenses, or almost any item in financial planning. "Cost of Goods Sold" is the amount of money that a company spends on manufacturing or purchasing items that it sells. This expense does not include salaries, overhead, and other routine expenses.

In addition to budgeted figures, a company will make preliminary or projected figures at the start of a year. In the following exercises you are asked to find percents of three departments for a year's budgeted and actual sales as well as projected sales for the following year.

EXERCISE 2: DETERMINING BUDGETED, ACTUAL, AND PROJECTED SALES

▶ The percent application problems are designed for you to apply what you have learned in the percent section. Should you need assistance as you complete these problems, you may refer back to the example percent problems. Notice that for Cost of Goods Sold, percents for each department are to be based on total sales. For this you must refer to Exercise 1. Gross Profit is the amount remaining after the Cost of Goods Sold is subtracted from total sales.

1. Budget Analysis

	Year: 1992 Budget	Percent of Total Sales	Year: 1992 Actual	Percent of Total Sales	Year 1993 Proj'd.	Percent of Total Sales
Income/Sales:						
Dept-A	$1,200,000	_____%	$1,224,000	_____%	$1,650,000	_____%
Dept-B	700,000	_____%	675,000	_____%	725,000	_____%
Dept-C	1,050,000	_____%	1,200,000	_____%	1,450,000	_____%
Total Sales:	$_____	100%	$_____	100%	$_____	100%

2. Cost of Goods Sold (COGS)

	Year: 1992 Budget	Percent of Total Sales	Year: 1992 Actual	Percent of Total Sales	Year 1993 Proj'd.	Percent of Total Sales
Dept-A	$501,000	_____%	$510,500	_____%	$830,000	_____%
Dept-B	425,000	_____%	410,000	_____%	485,000	_____%
Dept-C	730,000	_____%	740,000	_____%	780,000	_____%
Total COGS:	$_____	_____%	$_____	_____%	$_____	_____%
Gross Profit:	$_____	_____%	$_____	_____%	$_____	_____%

EXERCISE 3: COMPUTING INCREASES AND DECREASES

▶ Budget analysis includes the computation of increases and decreases in major categories. Then anticipated expenses are prorated for the next year.

Complete the table below. For "% Over/Under" use 1992 budget as the base. For the last column, "% Increase/Decrease" use 1992 actual as the base. Amounts are in thousands. That is, 700 stands for 700,000. Set your decimal selector at 2.

Dept.	1992 Budget	1992 Actual	Dollar Difference	% Over/ Under	1993 Projected	% Increase/ Decrease
A	$1,200	$1,224	$_____	_____%	$1,650	_____%
B	700	675	_____	_____%	725	_____%
C	1,050	1,200	_____	_____%	1,450	_____%
Total Sales	$_____ $_____		$_____	_____% $_____		_____%

▶ Prorate operating expenses by department.

Prorating of Operating Expenses
for 1993 Projected Budget
Based on Gross Sales per Department

	1993 Proj.	Dept. A 43%	Dept. B 19%	Dept. C 38%
Operating Expenses:				
Wages/Salaries	585	$_____	$_____	$_____
Executive Salaries	295	$_____	$_____	$_____
Rent	155	$_____	$_____	$_____
Utilities	120.5	$_____	$_____	$_____
Insurance	56.5	$_____	$_____	$_____
Office Supplies	37.3	$_____	$_____	$_____
Sales Commissions	285	$_____	$_____	$_____
Entertainment	12.5	$_____	$_____	$_____
Total Operating (Expenses)	_____	$_____	$_____	$_____

Lesson 17
TOUCH DRILL FOR SPEED DEVELOPMENT

1. _____
2. _____
3. _____
4. _____
5. _____
6. _____
7. _____
8. _____
9. _____
10. _____
11. _____
12. _____
13. _____
14. _____
15. _____
16. _____
17. _____
18. _____
19. _____
20. _____
21. _____
22. _____
23. _____
24. _____
25. _____
26. _____
27. _____
28. _____
29. _____
30. _____

▶ Calculate each sum. Record the total number of minutes and seconds it takes to complete this exercise on the line provided.

1.	465	2.	714	3.	901	4.	680
	231		285		307		403
	879		936		460		751
	645		915		210		102

5.	78,420	6.	12,068	7.	42,780	8.	64,071
	97,630		32,478		51,870		6,701
	85,620		20,498		63,470		58,021
	74,510		32,067		51,490		49,503

▶ Subtract.

9.	79,604	10.	82,017	11.	94,513	12.	63,906
	−31,460		−19,208		−16,025		−71,047

13.	581,002	14.	902,010	15.	120,805	16.	451,292
	−673,260		−102,390		− 70,410		−171,816

▶ Multiply. Set your decimal selector at 0.

17. 312 x 23   18. 714 x 14

19. 305 x 27   20. 825 x 35

21. 645 x 14   22. 404 x 30

▶ Find the sum for each problem below. Set your decimal selector at A. Remember that each entry must be a two-place decimal.

23.	927.04	24.	363.00	25.	96.01	26.	39.40
	120.03		131.00		714.06		217.04
	35.00		252.00		28.04		909.10
	91.03		858.00		302.08		302.14

27.	410.45	28.	501.29	29.	292.02	30.	503.76
	460.13		42.39		305.13		21.54
	585.05		805.12		432.40		797.07
	15.07		895.32		60.61		404.34

Lesson 17
APPLY YOUR SKILLS

▶ In addition to its cost of goods sold expense, a company must pay operating expenses. When all of a company's expenses are subtracted from its total revenue, the result is the profit. In the following exercises, you are asked to find each expense item as a percent of total sales. This is part of the same budget discussed previously. Total sales: 1992 budget, 2,950,000; 1992 actual, 3,099,000; 1993 projected, 3,825,000.

1. Find the total budgeted and actual and projected operating expenses. Then calculate each item as a percent of total sales.

OPERATING EXPENSES

	Year: 1992 Budget	Percent of Total Sales	Year: 1992 Actual	Percent of Total Sales	Year 1993 Proj'd.	Percent of Total Sales
Wages/ Salaries	$ 460,750	____%	$ 456,400	____%	$ 585,000	____%
Executive Salary	235,554	____%	242,500	____%	295,000	____%
Rent	131,664	____%	131,664	____%	155,000	____%
Utilities	97,725	____%	107,000	____%	120,500	____%
Insurance	37,878	____%	48,500	____%	56,480	____%
Office Supplies	29,950	____%	34,650	____%	37,300	____%
Sales Com- missions	195,000	____%	216,000	____%	285,000	____%
Entertainment	8,429	____%	10,380	____%	12,500	____%
Total Operating Expenses	$ ____	____%	$____	____%	$ ____	____%
Profit	$ 97,050	____%	$191,406	____%	$183,220	____%

2. The percents for the various columns above do not add up to 100%. What category of expenses, previously discussed, accounts for the missing amount? _____

3. Find the increase or decrease of the 1992 actual total expenses compared to budget. _____

4. Find the percent increase or decrease of the 1992 actual total expenses compared to budget. _____

Name _____

Lesson 17
CHECK YOUR PROGRESS

▶ Complete the table:

Department	Sales	Quota	Dollar Difference	Percent Over/Under Quota
A	$ 5,380	$_____	$ 465	_____
B	13,504	15,820	_____	_____
C	_____	4,926	(863)	_____
D	22,010	_____	1,380	_____
E	_____	16,444	(4,807)	_____
F	_____	8,360	25	_____
G	_____	_____	9,490	47.85
H	9,275	7,100	_____	_____
I	_____	6,350	895	_____
J	14,080	_____	(2,300)	_____
K	_____	_____	4,320	16.85
Total	$_____	$_____	$_____	_____

Lesson 17
MASTERY CHECKPOINT

▶ Allocate $64,300 in projected expenses based on the actual expenses listed. Find the percent for each expense category to one decimal place. Amounts are given in thousands.

	1992 Expenses	1993 Prorated Expenses	Percent
Operating Expenses:			
Wages/Salaries	$ 28.5	$_____	_____%
Executive Salaries	$ 12.1	$_____	_____%
Rent	$ 5.2	$_____	_____%
Utilities	$ 4.7	$_____	_____%
Insurance	$ 3.2	$_____	_____%
Office Supplies	$ 2.5	$_____	_____%
Sales Commissions	$ 10.4	$_____	_____%
Entertainment	$ 4.3	$_____	_____%
Total Operating Expenses	$____	$_____	_____%

Name _____

LESSON **18**

SIMPLE INTEREST

OBJECTIVES

After completing this lesson, you will be able to:

- Calculate simple interest when given principal, rate, and time.
- Calculate interest, principal, rate, or time when given the other three.

CALCULATING INTEREST

Interest is an amount of money paid for the use of money. When you put money in the bank, the bank pays interest to you. When you borrow money to buy a car or a house, you must pay interest on the amount you borrow. You pay back the amount borrowed, called the principal, and the interest over a period of months or years. When you do not pay the full amount charged on a credit card, you must pay interest on the unpaid balance.

Interest is calculated as a percent of the principal. If an amount is borrowed for a fixed period of time and paid back all at once, then the amount charged is called simple interest.

DEMONSTRATION EXAMPLE

If you borrowed $200 for one year at 12% interest and the entire loan was to be repaid in one payment, then at the end of a year you would pay the lender $200 plus the amount of interest. The interest would be $24:

$$200 \times 12\% = 24$$

EXERCISE 1: FINDING INTEREST

▶ Each of the following are single payment loans. They are to be repaid in full with interest after one year. Find the interest and total to be repaid.

	Amount borrowed	Interest rate	Interest	Total to be Repaid
1.	$100	10%	_____	_____
2.	$500	13%	_____	_____
3.	$250	12%	_____	_____
4.	$1,560	9%	_____	_____
5.	$708	10.5%	_____	_____

Name _____

THE TIME FACTOR

Usually money is not borrowed for exactly one year. Therefore, time must also be used in calculating interest. For simple interest, if you borrow an amount for two years, you must pay twice as much interest. If you borrow for 6 months, which is half a year, you pay half as much interest. To find interest, you multiply principal times rate times time.
$i = p \times r \times t$

DEMONSTRATION EXAMPLE

Find the interest on $2,500 borrowed for 2 years at 9% interest.

$i = p \times r \times t$

$i = 2,500 \times 0.09 \times 2 = 450$

The interest is $450

EXERCISE 2: USING TIME TO CALCULATE INTEREST

▶ Find the interest for given principle, rate, and time.

	Principal	x	Rate	x	Time (Years)	=	Interest
1.	$3,800		8%		3		_____
2.	$2,370		11.5%		4		_____
3.	$1,560		9.25%		2.5		_____
4.	$4,500		12.75%		1.25		_____
5.	$6,200		6.5%		3		_____
6.	$560		10%		0.5		_____
7.	$920		11.5%		1.5		_____

▶ The following are single payment loans. That is, the amount is to be repaid all at once. Find the interest and amount to be repaid. Set your decimal selector at 2.

	Principal	Rate	Time	Interest	Repayment
8.	$550	7%	1 yr	_____	_____
9.	$1,200	11%	2 yr	_____	_____
10.	$3,350	10.5%	3 yr	_____	_____
11.	$5,890	12.5%	2.5 yr	_____	_____
12.	$3,125	9.5%	0.5 yr	_____	_____
13.	$6,000	10%	5 yr	_____	_____
14.	$8,500	8%	3.5 yr	_____	_____
15.	$4,790	12.5%	2 yr	_____	_____

Simple interest for less than a year is sometimes based on a "banker's year," which is 360 days. When using the banker's year, simple interest can be calculated for any number of days by using the following formula:

$$\text{Simple interest} = \frac{\text{Principal x Rate x Time (in days)}}{\text{Days per year (360)}}$$

DEMONSTRATION EXAMPLE

$5,000 is loaned at 7% interest for 85 days.

$$\text{Simple interest} = \frac{\text{Principal x Rate x Time}}{\text{Days per year}}$$

$$= \frac{5,000 \times 7\% \times 85}{360}$$

$$= 82.64$$

Name _____

EXERCISE 3: USING THE BANKER'S YEAR

▶ Use the banker's year (360 days) for the following simple interest problems.

	Principal	Rate	Time	Interest	Repayment
1.	$650.00	9.00%	90	$_____	$_____
2.	$935.00	9.25%	120	$_____	$_____
3.	$1,026.49	9.50%	210	$_____	$_____
4.	$1,225.80	8.75%	195	$_____	$_____
5.	$1,986.31	9.75%	320	$_____	$_____
6.	$2,493.67	10.25%	119	$_____	$_____
7.	$3,500.00	9.33%	350	$_____	$_____
8.	$5,150.0	9.50%	305	$_____	$_____
9.	$6,230.00	10.50%	211	$_____	$_____
10.	$8,437.12	11.00%	343	$_____	$_____
11.	$9,680.95	9 3/4%	150	$_____	$_____
12.	$7,083.00	9 1/4%	110	$_____	$_____
13.	$1,540.00	9 3/4%	240	$_____	$_____
14.	$862.49	11 2/3%	30	$_____	$_____
15.	$500.00	10 1/2%	90	$_____	$_____

Lesson 18
APPLY YOUR SKILLS

The formula for finding interest can also be used to find any of the other variables: principal, rate, or time. If you know three out of the four, then you can find the missing quantity.

DEMONSTRATION EXAMPLE

Find the rate on $2,500 if the interest for 3.5 years is $918.75. Use the simple interest formula:

Interest	=	Principal	x	Rate	x	Time
918.75	=	2,500	x	r	x	3.5

$$\frac{918.75}{(3.5 \times 2,500)} = r$$

Enter:	918.75	÷		3.5	÷		2,500	%
Display:	918.75	918.75		3.5	262.5		2,500	10.5

The interest rate is 10.5%.

The following information is for different loans. Solve each for the unknown term.

	Interest	=	Principal	x	Rate	x	Time (Years)
1.	$1,100		$5,000		_____		2
2.	$712.50		$3,000		9.5%		_____
3.	$586.50		$_____		11.5%		1
4.	$_____		$2,230		12.25%		1.5
5.	$690		$_____		8%		2.5
6.	$136.90		$740		18.5%		_____
7.	$15,962.50		$25,000		_____		5
8.	$1,050		$20,000		_____		0.5
9.	$_____		$11,200		6.5%		6
10.	$3,403.125		$16,500		_____		2.5

Name _____

Lesson 18
CHECK YOUR PROGRESS

▶ Find the interest for the given principle, rate, and time.

	Interest	=	Principal	x	Rate	x	Time (Years)
1.	_____		$2,900		6%		2
2.	_____		$4,300		9.5%		3
3.	_____		$915		18.5%		1
4.	_____		$3,800		10.75%		3.5
5.	_____		$7,700		13.25%		4

	Interest	=	Principal	x	Rate	x	Time (Days)
6.	_____		$12,210		11.5%		120
7.	_____		$1,760		14.5%		90
8.	_____		$728		21%		180
9.	_____		$516.98		20.5%		200
10.	_____		$21,876.45		18.5%		270

Lesson 18
MASTERY CHECKPOINT

▶ Solve each of the following for the unknown term.

	Interest =	Principal x	Rate x	Time (Years)
1.	$648	_____	12%	2
2.	$354.38	$1,350	_____	2.5
3.	_____	$1,900	6.5%	5
4.	$6,440	$14,000	11.5%	_____
5.	$351.90	$782	_____	2.5
6.	$5,512.50	$ 9,000	12.25%	_____
7.	$596.63	_____	21.5%	1.5
8.	_____	$3,775	13.25%	3
9.	$138.74	$562	_____	1.25
10.	$713.36	_____	20.25%	2.75

Name _____

COMPOUND INTEREST

After completing this lesson, you will be able to:

- Calculate compound interest based on principal, rate, and time.
- Calculate the number of years needed to double or triple an investment based on a given interest rate.

WORKING WITH COMPOUND INTEREST

When you invest money in a bank, the interest is added to the principal on a regular basis. Additional interest is then based on this new principal. This method is called "compound interest." The amount of your interest does not remain the same—as it would for simple interest—but keeps increasing because the principal keeps increasing.

To work with compound interest, you will need to use exponents. An exponent is simply a raised number that tells you to multiply a base number by itself so many times.

DEMONSTRATION EXAMPLE 1

Find   (a) 2^5; (b) 1.07^9

$$(a) \ 2^5 = 2 \times 2 \times 2 \times 2 \times 2 = 32$$

On your business calculator, this repetition can be done by repeated use of the $\boxed{=}$ or $\boxed{\text{x}}$ key or by using the constant function. Check your calculator manual or ask your instructor for assistance.

$$(b) \ 1.07^9 = 1.8386$$

Suppose you invest $100 for 2 years at 8% interest compounded annually. The interest for one year is $8. The new principal at the end of the year is the principal plus the interest, which is $108. The interest for the second year is $108 \times 0.08 = 8.64$, and the new principal is $108 + 8.64 = 116.64$.

Since interest is computed as a percent of principal, you can think of the principal as 100% and add the interest rate. Then the amount to be paid can be found in one step. For example, if you invest $500 for one year at 9%, you can find the total amount of principal plus interest as follows:

$$500 \times 1.09 = 545$$

When interest is compounded every year, each new principal is multiplied again by 100% plus the interest rate.

DEMONSTRATION EXAMPLE 2

Find the growth of $1,000 invested at 9% compounded annually for 5 years.

$$1{,}000 \ (1.09)^5 = 1{,}000 \times 1.5386 = 1{,}538.62$$

$1,000 invested for 5 years at 9% interest will grow to $1,538.62.

EXERCISE 1: DETERMINING COMPOUND INTEREST

▶ Find the amount of each number raised to the given exponent. Give each answer to four decimal places.

1. $5^{10} =$ _____

2. $4.8^6 =$ _____

3. $1.57^{20} =$ _____

4. $1.095^{25} =$ _____

5. $2.3^9 =$ _____

6. $1.02^{30} =$ _____

7. $1.075^{15} =$ _____

8. $6.8^5 =$ _____

9. $1.06^{10} =$ _____

10. $1.055^{10} =$ _____

▶ Find the amount each investment compounded yearly at the given rate and after the given number of years.

	Investment	Rate	Time (in Years)	Amount
11.	$100	8%	4	_____
12.	$1,000	8.5%	7	_____
13.	$385	10%	10	_____
14.	$760.50	6.5%	20	_____
15.	$1,340	9.25%	8	_____
16.	$3,590.40	11.5%	15	_____
17.	$100	10.5%	7	_____
18.	$1,000	5.5%	13	_____
19.	$5,690	14.6%	6	_____
20.	$2,287.61	9.17%	11	_____
21.	$10,000	6%	12	_____
22.	$6,812	7.55%	10	_____
23.	$3,014.50	8.47%	20	_____
24.	$100	10.5%	14	_____
25.	$800	5.5%	26	_____

1. DETERMINING COMPOUND INTEREST

1. _____
2. _____
3. _____
4. _____
5. _____
6. _____
7. _____
8. _____
9. _____
10. _____
11. _____
12. _____
13. _____
14. _____
15. _____
16. _____
17. _____
18. _____
19. _____
20. _____
21. _____
22. _____
23. _____
24. _____
25. _____

Name _____

INTEREST TABLES

Bankers and others who work on investments frequently use tables to make quick calculations. The following table shows principal and interest on $1 for different interest rates and different numbers of years. Entries have six decimal places because sometimes very large amounts are invested.

Growth of $1 at Compound Interest

Periods	5%	6%	7%	8%	9%	10%
1	1.050 000	1.060 000	1.070 000	1.080 000	1.090 000	1.100 000
2	1.102 500	1.123 600	1.144 900	1.166 400	1.188 100	1.210 000
3	1.157 625	1.191 016	1.225 043	1.259 712	1.295 029	1.331 000
4	1.215 506	1.262 477	1.310 796	1.360 489	1.411 582	1.464 100
5	1 276 282	1.338 226	1.402 552	1.469 328	1.538 624	1.610 510
6	1.340 096	1.418 519	1.500 730	1.586 874	1.677 100	1.771 561
7	1.407 100	1.503 630	1.605 781	1.713 824	1.828 039	1.948 717
8	1.477 455	1.593 848	1.718 186	1.850 930	1.992 563	2.143 589
9	1.551 328	1.689 479	1.838 459	1.999 005	2.171 893	2.357 948
10	1.628 895	1.790 848	1.967 151	2.158 925	2.367 364	2.593 742
11	1.710 339	1.898 299	2.104 852	2.331 639	2.580 426	2.853 117
12	1.795 856	2.012 196	2.252 192	2.518 170	2.812 665	3.138 428
13	1.885 649	2.132 928	2.409 845	2.719 624	3.065 805	3.452 271
14	1.979 932	2.260 904	2.578 534	2.937 194	3.341 727	3.797 498
15	2.078 928	2.396 558	2.759 032	3.172 169	3.642 482	4.177 248
16	2.182 875	2.540 352	2.952 164	3.425 943	3.970 306	4.594 973
17	2.292 018	2.692 773	3.158 815	3.700 018	4.327 633	5.054 470
18	2.406 619	2.854 339	3.379 932	3.996 019	4.717 120	5.559 917
19	2.526 950	3.025 600	3.616 528	4.315 701	5.141 661	6.115 909
20	2.653 298	3.207 135	3.869 684	4.660 957	5.604 411	6.727 500

Figure 19.1.   Compound interest table

DEMONSTRATION EXAMPLE

An insurance company invests $682,000 at 8% compounded annually. Find the amount of this investment after 15 years. To find the amount of growth on $1, look at the interest table for the 8% column and the 15-year row. The number where this column and row meet is: 3.172169. To find the growth of the amount invested: 682,000 x 3.172169 = 2,163,419.26. After 15 years the investment will equal $2,163,419.26.

EXERCISE 2: USING INTEREST TABLES

▶ Use the interest table (Figure 19.1) to find the amount of each investment after the given number of years compounded annually.

1. $1,000 for 10 years at 9%   2. $4,600 for 18 years at 6%

_____   _____

3. $15,000 for 6 years at 10%   4. $20,500 for 20 years at 7%

_____   _____

5. $43,000 for 12 years at 5%   6. $125,000 for 11 years at 9%

_____   _____

7. $35,800 for 16 years at 9%   8. $120,000 for 17 years at 6%

_____   _____

9. $2,000,000 for 10 years at 10%   10. $4,560,000 for 20 years at 8%

_____   _____

Name _____

1. _____
2. _____
3. _____
4. _____
5. _____
6. _____
7. _____
8. _____
9. _____
10. _____
11. _____

Lesson 19
APPLY YOUR SKILLS

When making long-term investments, people often ask how long it will take to double their money. This can be useful information—particularly when planning for a child's education, for retirement, or for paying a debt that will come due some years in the future. You can find out how long it will take to double an amount of money by considering an investment of one dollar. Using the formula for compound interest, the doubling time will be when the investment of one dollar equals two dollars.

DEMONSTRATION EXAMPLE

How many years will it take for an amount of money to double when invested at 6.6% interest compounded annually?

To find this answer, you must find the exponent n that satisfies the equation $1.066^n = 2$. The answer need not be exact, but it should be close to 2. The solution is found by using the $\boxed{\times}$ or $\boxed{=}$ key and counting as the repeated multiplication gives answers approaching 2. Try this and you will find $1.066^{11} = 2.02$. Money invested at 6.6% will, therefore, double in 11 years.

▶ Find out approximately how long it will take to double your money at each of the given rates.

1. 4.5% _____   2. 10% _____

3. 7.5% _____   4. 11.5% _____

5. 8.25% _____   6. 15% _____

7. If you double your investment in 8 years at a given rate, what will happen to your investment in 16 years?_____

8. If you triple your investment in 12 years at a given rate, what will happen to your investment in 24 years? _____

Use trial and error with your calculator and the compound investment formula to answer the following.

9. What interest rate will triple your money in 12 years?

_____

10. What interest rate will turn $1,000 into $1,800 in 6 years?

_____

11. If $10,000 is invested at 11% for 10 years, how much greater will be the final amount be than if it is invested at 9%? _____

Lesson 19
CHECK YOUR PROGRESS

▶ Find the amount of each number raised to the given power. Give each answer to two decimal places.

1. $7^{10} = $ _____

2. $3.9^7 = $ _____

3. $1.03^{18} = $ _____

4. $1.085^{22} = $ _____

▶ Find the amount of each investment compounded annually at the given rate and after the given number of years.

	Investment	Rate	Time (in years)	Amount
5.	$950	9%	6	_____
6.	$1,680	10.5%	7	_____
7.	$6,348	5.55%	10	_____
8.	$4,320	7.88%	15	_____

▶ Find the interest rate needed for each of the following amounts to reach $1,000 in 10 years.

9. $500 _____

10. $600 _____

CHECK YOUR
PROGRESS

1. _____
2. _____
3. _____
4. _____
5. _____
6. _____
7. _____
8. _____
9. _____
10. _____

Name _____

1. _____

2. _____

3. _____

4. _____

5. _____

6. _____

7. _____

8. _____

9. _____

10. _____

Lesson 19
MASTERY CHECKPOINT

▶ Find the amount of each investment compounded annually at the given rate and after the given number of years.

	Investment	Rate	Time (in years)	Amount
1.	$782	7.5%	7	_____
2.	$2,600	12.25%	10	_____
3.	$4,700	6.75%	25	_____
4.	$408.65	10.68%	18	_____

▶ Find the time needed to double your money at each rate.

5. 8.2% _____   6. 10.6% _____

7. 12.3% _____   8. 5.8% _____

▶ Find the interest rate for the following amounts to reach $1,000 in 5 years.

9. $700 _____   10. $400 _____

TRUE ANNUAL INTEREST RATE

OBJECTIVES

After completing this lesson you will be able to:

- Calculate the total interest paid on an installment purchase.
- Calculate the true annual interest rate.

INSTALLMENT PURCHASES

An installment purchase means that you buy an item and pay for it in a number of equal amounts—usually made on a monthly basis. Interest on installment purchases may be calculated on the entire price of the item. Or you may be told to pay a certain amount for a given number of months. One thing that most people purchase on an installment basis is a car. But many other household and business items are also purchased in this way.

DEMONSTRATION EXAMPLE 1

Find the interest amount on a 3-year car loan of $4,500 with an interest rate of 11% on the principal.

Interest	=	Principal	x	Rate	x	Time		
	=	4,500	x	11%	x	3	=	1,485

EXERCISE 1: DETERMINING TOTAL INTEREST FOR INSTALLMENT PURCHASES

▶ Find the total interest for each amount. Remember, there are 12 months in a year. (15 months ÷ 12 months = 1.25 years)

1. $900 at 10% for 1 year.

2. $2,000 at 8% for 1.5 years.

3. $2,800 at 9.5% for 2 years.

4. $5,000 at 11% for 3.5 years.

5. $3,796 at 12.25% for 2.5 years.

6. $6,440 at 9.5% for 21 months.

7. $870 at 10.5% for 15 months.

8. $670 at 11.25% for 6 months.

9. $450 at 8.5% for 3 months.

10. $1,235 at 10% for 2 years.

1. _____
2. _____
3. _____
4. _____
5. _____
6. _____
7. _____
8. _____
9. _____
10. _____

Once you know the total amount of interest for a loan, you add this amount to the principal and divide the total by the number of months to find the monthly payment.

DEMONSTRATION EXAMPLE 2

Find the monthly payment on an installment loan of $2,400 at 9.5% to be paid over 2.5 years. First find the total amount of interest.

Interest =	Principal	x	Rate	x	Time	
=	2,400	x	9.5%	x	2.5	= 570

Find the total to be paid and divide to find the monthly payments.

To find the number of months: 2.5 x 12 = 30

Keystrokes:	2,400	➕	570	＝	➗	30
Display:	2,400	2,400	570	2970	2,970	99

The monthly payment is $99.

Name_____

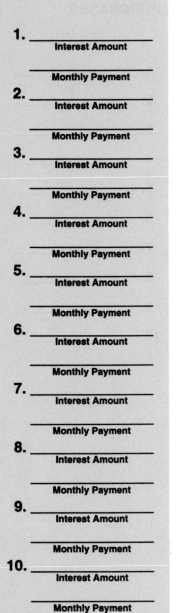

2. DETERMINING MONTHLY PAYMENT

1. _____
Interest Amount

_____
Monthly Payment

2. _____
Interest Amount

_____
Monthly Payment

3. _____
Interest Amount

_____
Monthly Payment

4. _____
Interest Amount

_____
Monthly Payment

5. _____
Interest Amount

_____
Monthly Payment

6. _____
Interest Amount

_____
Monthly Payment

7. _____
Interest Amount

_____
Monthly Payment

8. _____
Interest Amount

_____
Monthly Payment

9. _____
Interest Amount

_____
Monthly Payment

10. _____
Interest Amount

_____
Monthly Payment

EXERCISE 2: DETERMINING MONTHLY PAYMENT

Find the total interest and monthly payment for each.

1. $500 at 10% for 1 year.

   Interest amount _____

   Monthly payment _____

2. $1,250 at 11% for 2 years.

   Interest amount _____

   Monthly payment _____

3. $2,500 at 11.5% for 2.5 years.

   Interest amount _____

   Monthly payment _____

4. $4,650 at 9.5% for 3.5 years.

   Interest amount _____

   Monthly payment _____

5. $895 at 8.5% for 15 months.

   Interest amount _____

   Monthly payment _____

6. $1,368 at 11.25% for 21 months.

   Interest amount _____

   Monthly payment _____

7. $1,768 at 12% for 30 months.

   Interest amount _____

   Monthly payment _____

8. $6,000 at 12.6% for 3.5 years.

   Interest amount _____

   Monthly payment _____

9. $505 at 8.6% for 6 months.

   Interest amount _____

   Monthly payment _____

10. $423.50 at 10.25% for 9 months.

    Interest amount _____

    Monthly payment _____

As you pay off a loan or make installment purchases, the principal decreases. Suppose you borrow $1,000 for a year with an interest charge of $100. This appears to be 10% interest. But that interest is for the use of the entire principal for one year. If you make monthly payments to repay the loan, then you do not have the use of the $1,000 for the whole year. So the $100 really represents an interest rate higher than 10%. Lending institutions are generally required to tell borrowers the true annual interest rate. This rate can be calculated using the following formula.

$$\text{True annual interest rate} = \frac{24 \times \text{Interest amount}}{\text{Principal} \times (\text{Number of payments} + 1)}$$

DEMONSTRATION EXAMPLE 3

Find the true annual interest rate on $2,400 borrowed for 2.5 years at 10.5%.

Interest amount = 2,400 x 10.5% x 2.5 = 630

Number of payments = 2.5 x 12 = 30

$$\text{True annual interest rate} = \frac{24 \times 630}{2,400 \times 31}$$

Enter:	24	$\boxed{x}$	630	$\boxed{\div}$	2,400	$\boxed{\div}$	31	$\boxed{\%}$
Display:	24	24	630	15,120	2,400	6.3	31	20.32

EXERCISE 3: FINDING THE TRUE ANNUAL INTEREST RATE

▶ Find the interest amount, the monthly payment, and the true annual interest rate for each of the following:

1. Principal $500   Interest rate 9%

    Total number of payments 12 (360 days)

    Interest amount   _____

    Monthly payment   _____

    Annual interest rate   _____

2. Principal $675   Interest rate 10%

    Total number of payments 15 (450 days)

    Interest amount   _____

    Monthly payment   _____

    Annual interest rate   _____

3. Principal $850   Interest rate 11%

    Total number of payments 18 (540 days)

    Interest amount   _____

    Monthly payment   _____

    Annual interest rate   _____

4. Principal $1,000   Interest rate 9%

    Total number of payments 24 (720 days)

    Interest amount   _____

    Monthly payment   _____

    Annual interest rate   _____

5. Principal $1,500   Interest rate 8%

    Total number of payments 30 (900 days)

    Interest amount   _____

    Monthly payment   _____

    Annual interest rate   _____

6. Principal $1,350   Interest rate 10%

    Total number of payments 14 (420 days)

    Interest amount   _____

    Monthly payment   _____

    Annual interest rate   _____

3. FINDING THE TRUE ANNUAL INTEREST RATE

1. _____
   Interest Amount

   _____
   Monthly Payment

   _____
   Annual Interest Rate

2. _____
   Interest Amount

   _____
   Monthly Payment

   _____
   Annual Interest Rate

3. _____
   Interest Amount

   _____
   Monthly Payment

   _____
   Annual Interest Rate

4. _____
   Interest Amount

   _____
   Monthly Payment

   _____
   Annual Interest Rate

5. _____
   Interest Amount

   _____
   Monthly Payment

   _____
   Annual Interest Rate

6. _____
   Interest Amount

   _____
   Monthly Payment

   _____
   Annual Interest Rate

Name_____

MORTGAGE PAYMENTS

For mortgage payments on a house and for many other loans, the interest is based on the unpaid balance of the loan. But to make payments simpler for the borrower, a method is used that provides equal monthly payments. A part of each payment goes to reduce the principal amount borrowed, and a part is the interest payment. When payments begin, payment on the principal is small, but the interest is large. As time passes the principal payment increases while the interest becomes smaller. But the interest rate remains the same. The table below illustrates monthly payment amounts on $1,000 borrowed for different numbers of years at different interest rates.

Monthly Mortgage Payment per $1,000

Years	7.5%	8%	8.5%	9%	9.5%	10%
15	8.27	9.56	9.85	10.14	10.44	10.75
20	8.06	8.36	8.68	9.00	9.32	9.65
25	7.39	7.72	8.05	8.39	8.74	9.09
30	6.99	7.34	7.69	8.05	8.41	8.78

DEMONSTRATION EXAMPLE 1

Find the monthly payment on a $75,000 mortgage for 20 years at 8.5% interest.

Reading the table down to 20 years and across to 8.5%, we find 8.68. This is the monthly payment on $1,000. To find the payment for $75,000, multiply 8.68 by 75:

75 x $8.68 = $651. The monthly payment will be $651.

DEMONSTRATION EXAMPLE 2

Find the total amount of principal and interest paid on a loan of $90,000 at 9.5% for 25 years.

The monthly amount for $1,000 is $8.74

The monthly payment on $90,000: 90 x $8.74 = $786.60

There are 12 months in a year. The number of payments is 12 x 25

Total amount paid is: 12 x 25 x $786.60 = $235,980.

1. Find the monthly payment on
   $60,000 for 30 years at 8%.

   _____

2. Find the monthly payment on
   $40,000 for 15 years at 10%.

   _____

3. Find the total amount of
   principal and interest paid
   on $70,000 for 20 years at 9%.

   _____

4. Find the total amount paid
   on a $55,000 mortgage for
   30 years at 9.5%.

   _____

5. Find the amount of interest
   paid on $45,000 for 15 years at 8%.

   _____

6. Find the amount of interest paid
   on $90,000 for 30 years at 10.5%.

   _____

1. _____

2. _____

3. _____

4. _____

5. _____

6. _____

Name_____

Lesson 20
APPLY YOUR SKILLS

1. Find the total interest on $5,600 at 9.5% for 4 years.

_____

2. Find the monthly payment on $1,800 at 10% for 3 years.

_____

3. Find the total interest on $2,220 at 11.5% for 2.5 years.

_____

4. Find the monthly payment on $896 at 10.5% for 6 months.

_____

5. Find the true annual interest rate on $1,302 at 10% for 2 years.

_____

6. Find the true annual interest on $564 at 18% for 1 year.

_____

7. Find the monthly payment on $4,750 at 12% for 5 years.

_____

8. Find the monthly payment on $1,558 at 14% for 3 years.

_____

9. Find the true annual interest rate on $3,260 at 11.75% with 30 payments.

_____

10. Find the true annual interest on $456.92 at 21% with 15 payments.

_____

▶ For each of the following, find the interest amount, the monthly payment, and the true annual interest rate.

	Principal	Rate	Number of Payments	Interest Amount	Monthly Payment	True Annual Interest Rate
11.	$312.76	11.6%	15	_____	_____	_____
12.	$785.01	20.5%	27	_____	_____	_____
13.	$901.67	18.75%	30	_____	_____	_____
14.	$478.10	15.3%	20	_____	_____	_____
15.	$309.78	10.2%	12	_____	_____	_____

Lesson 20
CHECK YOUR PROGRESS

▶ Find the total interest for each amount. Remember, there are 12 months in a year (15 months ÷ 12 months = 1.25 years).

1. $1,200 at 9% for 1 year.

2. $2,680 at 7% for 1.5 years.

_____

_____

3. $610 at 9.5% for 3 years.

4. $1,850 at 11.5% for 2.5 years.

_____

_____

▶ Find the total interest and monthly payment for each of the following:

5. $350 at 13% for 1 year.

Interest amount _____

Monthly payment _____

6. $1,350 at 18% for 2 years.

Interest amount _____

Monthly payment _____

7. Principal $275   Interest rate 12%

Total number of payments 12 (360 days)

Interest amount   _____

Monthly payment   _____

Annual interest rate   _____

8. Principal $125   Interest rate 11%

Total number of payments 8 (240 days)

Interest amount   _____

Monthly payment   _____

Annual interest rate   _____

Name_____

Lesson 20
MASTERY CHECKPOINT

▶ Find the total interest for each amount.

1. $850 at 19% for 1 year.

   _____

2. $1,900 at 13.5% for 3 years.

   _____

3. $6,510 at 2.5% for 4 years

   _____

4. $805 at 11.5% for 1.5 years.

   _____

▶ Find the total interest and monthly payment for each amount.

5. $350 at 21% for 1 year.

   Interest amount _____

   Monthly payment _____

6. $5,560 at 2.9% for 4 years.

   Interest amount _____

   Monthly payment _____

7. Principal $50   Interest rate 9%

   Total number of payments 4 (120 days)

   Interest amount   _____

   Monthly payment   _____

   Annual interest rate   _____

8. Principal $360   Interest rate 13%

   Total number of payments 20 (600 days)

   Interest amount   _____

   Monthly payment   _____

   Annual interest rate   _____

THE INCOME STATEMENT

OBJECTIVES

After completing this lesson you will be able to:

- Read and interpret an income statement.
- Calculate income (profit) for an income statement.

UNDERSTANDING INCOME STATEMENTS

The income statement is one of the most important financial statements prepared by an accountant for a company. The income statement tells the managers and owners of the company how well the company has done during a certain time period. This time is usually one month, three months, six months, or a year.

The major categories found on an income statement are:

Revenue—amount received from the sale of merchandise or services.

Cost of goods sold (COGS)—amount spent for merchandise sold.

Gross profit on sales—the amount remaining after the COGS has been subtracted from the revenue.

Operating expenses—amount spent for the goods and services needed to operate a business.

Net income or Net profit—the amount remaining after operating expenses have been subtracted from gross profit on sales.

DEMONSTRATION EXAMPLE

The Emax Company has the following finances: Revenue, $104,300; COGS, $51,600; operating expenses, $39,700. Write an abbreviated income statement by finding the gross profit on sales and the net income.

Revenue	104,300
COGS	− 51,600
Gross profit	52,700
Operating expense	− 39,700
Net income	13,000

EXERCISE 1: WRITING ABBREVIATED INCOME STATEMENTS

▶ Complete each of the following abbreviated income statements.

1. Revenue   108,900
   COGS   59,200
   Gross profit   _____
   Operating expenses   41,300
   Net income   _____

2. Revenue   376,100
   COGS   184,700
   Gross profit   _____
   Operating expenses   124,500
   Net income   _____

3. Revenue   723,100
   COGS   308,611
   Gross profit   _____
   Operating expenses   367,600
   Net income   _____

4. Revenue   671,200
   COGS   461,200
   Gross profit   _____
   Operating expenses   176,300
   Net income   _____

5. Revenue   402,128
   COGS   292,801
   Gross profit   _____
   Operating expenses   90,168
   Net income   _____

6. Revenue   921,050
   COGS   501,273
   Gross profit   _____
   Operating expenses   341,040
   Net income   _____

7. Revenue   778,000
   COGS   307,126
   Gross profit   _____
   Operating expenses   241,890
   Net income   _____

8. Revenue   502,130
   COGS   389,201
   Gross profit   _____
   Operating expenses   137,208
   Net income   _____

9. Revenue   902,151
   COGS   584,230
   Gross profit   _____
   Operating expenses   167,003
   Net income   _____

10. Revenue   783,228
    COGS   320,184
    Gross profit   _____
    Operating expenses 286,510
    Net income   _____

Name _____

COMPLETING INCOME STATEMENTS

A sample income statement is shown below. The final figures in each category are carried in the second column. Income statements do not show whether an item is being added or subtracted. You must know this.

EXERCISE 2: CALCULATING PERCENT OF NET SALES

▶ Check the addition and subtraction on the sample statement. Then calculate each item as a percent of net sales. This is not part of the income statement.

BELGO'S HOME FURNISHINGS

INCOME STATEMENT

For the Quarter Ended June 30, 1992

			Percent of Net Sales
Revenue:			
Sales	$385,700		
Less: Returns	21,800		
Net sales		$363,900	
Cost of goods sold:			
Merchandise inventory, April 1	$168,300		1. _____
Purchases	78,200		2. _____
COG available for sale, April 1	$246,500		3. _____
Less: Mdse Inv., June 30	65,800		4. _____
Cost of goods sold		180,700	5. _____
Gross profit......................................		183,200	6. _____
Operating expenses:			
Salaries expense	$104,600		7. _____
Supplies expense	8,300		8. _____
Office expense	6,400		9. _____
Utilities expense..........................	9,200		10. _____
Miscellaneous expense	5,900		11. _____
Total operating expense		134,400	12. _____
Net income		48,800	13. _____

Name _____

EXERCISE 3: CALCULATING THE PARTS OF AN INCOME STATEMENT

▶ For the following income statement, calculate the net sales, cost of goods sold, gross profit, operating expenses, and net income. Then calculate each item as a percent of net sales.

BELGO'S HOME FURNISHINGS
INCOME STATEMENT
For the Quarter Ended September 1992

		Percent of Net Sales
Revenue:		
Sales	$295,700	
Less: Returns	16,000	
Net sales	_____	
Cost of goods sold:		
Merchandise inventory, July 1	$108,500	1. _____
Purchases	57,300	2. _____
COG available for sale, July 1	$165,800	3. _____
Less: Mdse Inv., Sept. 30 ...	39,100	4. _____
Cost of goods sold	_____	5. _____
Gross profit	_____	6. _____
Operating expenses:		
Salaries expense	$ 92,100	7. _____
Supplies expense...................	6,800	8. _____
Office expense	5,300	9. _____
Utilities expense	8,700	10. _____
Miscellaneous expense...........	4,200	11. _____
Total operating expense	_____	12. _____
Net income................................	_____	13. _____

Lesson 21

TOUCH DRILL FOR SPEED DEVELOPMENT

▶ Calculate each sum. Record the total number of minutes and seconds it takes to complete these exercises on the line provided.

1.	195	2.	486	3.	209	4.	701
	737		256		130		208
	493		845		760		903
	671		927		505		290

5.	79,132	6.	96,803	7.	80,914	8.	89,573
	31,897		10,758		76,534		19,703
	20,564		39,014		80,694		26,481
	30,714		67,902		10,231		38,602

▶ Subtract.

9.	75,902	10.	40,781	11.	98,990	12.	67,034
	−20,638		−38,905		−14,585		−12,345

13.	674,008	14.	908,706	15.	674,020	16.	905,434
	−105,749		−120,403		− 98,562		−673,020

▶ Multiply. Set your decimal selector at 0.

17.	129 x 35	18.	307 x 45
19.	617 x 55	20.	175 x 65
21.	209 x 75	22.	678 x 85

▶ Find the sum for each problem below. Set your decimal selector at A. Remember that each entry must be a two-place decimal.

23.	564.90	24.	812.60	25.	57.11	26.	70.03
	206.54		735.68		877.09		142.05
	78.00		124.76		88.45		731.00
	35.07		689.01		606.01		205.67

27.	176.00	28.	908.71	29.	102.00	30.	612.00
	875.00		67.00		874.00		65.08
	651.00		182.03		102.08		753.88
	13.00		904.57		50.06		494.00

1. _____
2. _____
3. _____
4. _____
5. _____
6. _____
7. _____
8. _____
9. _____
10. _____
11. _____
12. _____
13. _____
14. _____
15. _____
16. _____
17. _____
18. _____
19. _____
20. _____
21. _____
22. _____
23. _____
24. _____
25. _____
26. _____
27. _____
28. _____
29. _____
30. _____

Name _____

Lesson 21
APPLY YOUR SKILLS

▶ Belgo's year-end sales were $1,138,500. Returns were $70,300. Merchandise inventory on Jan. 1 was $175,200. Purchases were $438,100. Merchandise inventory on Dec. 31 was $95,600. Use the sample income statement in the lesson and the figures below to complete the income statement. Calculate each amount as a percent of net sales.

BELGO'S HOME FURNISHINGS

INCOME STATEMENT

For the Year Ended December 1992

Revenue:			Percent of Net Sales
Sales	_____		
Less: Returns	_____		
Net sales		_____	
Cost of goods sold:			
Merchandise Inventory, Jan. 1	_____		1. _____
Purchases	_____		2. _____
COG available for sale, Jan. 1		_____	3. _____
Less: Mdse Inv., Dec. 31	_____		4. _____
Cost of goods sold		_____	5. _____
Gross profit		_____	6. _____
Operating expenses:			
Salaries expense	$403,200		7. _____
Supplies expense....................	25,300		8. _____
Office expense	19,200		9. _____
Utilities expense	34,700		10. _____
Miscellaneous expense...........	18,500		11. _____
Total operating expense		_____	12. _____
Net income		_____	13. _____

Lesson 21
CHECK YOUR PROGRESS

▶ Complete the abbreviated income statements for each of the following.

1. Revenue   784,300
   COGS   <u>302,700</u>
   Gross profit   _____
   Operating expenses <u>143,900</u>
   Net income   _____

2. Revenue   265,400
   COGS   <u>187,200</u>
   Gross profit   _____
   Operating expenses <u>74,200</u>
   Net income   _____

3. Revenue   504,100
   COGS   <u>231,200</u>
   Gross profit   _____
   Operating expenses <u>176,400</u>
   Net income   _____

4. Revenue   439,200
   COGS   <u>256,500</u>
   Gross profit   _____
   Operating expenses <u>108,600</u>
   Net income   _____

Name _____

Lesson 21
MASTERY CHECKPOINT

▶ Sales for the Book Palace were $265,400; returns were $16,300. Merchandise inventory on Jan. 1 was $31,700. Purchases were $182,400. Merchandise inventory on Dec. 31 was $24,700. Use this information to complete the partial income statement below.

THE BOOK PALACE

INCOME STATEMENT

For the Quarter Ended December 1992

			Percent of Net Sales
Revenue:			
Sales	_____		
Less: Returns	_____		
Net sales		_____	
Cost of goods sold:			
Merchandise Inventory, Jan. 1	_____		1. _____
Purchases	_____		2. _____
COG available for sale, Jan. 1	_____		3. _____
Less: Mdse Inv., Dec. 31	_____		4. _____
Cost of goods sold		_____	5. _____
Gross profit		_____	6. _____

THE BALANCE SHEET

OBJECTIVES

After completing this lesson you will be able to:

- Define assets, liabilities, and owner's equity.
- Balance the accounting equation.
- Complete four-column accounting forms.

THE OVERALL FINANCIAL PICTURE

In the previous lesson we considered sales and expenses as they are presented in the income statement. The income statement tells how a business has done during a particular time—such as a month or a year. But business owners and managers also like to consider the general financial condition of a company at a particular point in time.

To present an overall financial picture, a business uses a form called a "balance sheet." There are three main categories on a balance sheet: assets, liabilities, and owner's equity. These are defined as follows:

Assets—things of value owned by a business.

Liabilities—debts owed by a business.

Owner's equity—the difference between assets and liabilities.

There are different kinds of assets that belong to a company. Buildings, equipment, furniture, and inventory or merchandise for sale are the most common kinds of assets. An abbreviated balance sheet is shown in Figure 22.1. It is for a business that makes copies and does faxing for customers. This company has just started. Cash means money that the company has in the bank. The company has some debts because of

Quick Copy Center
Balance Sheet
April 30, 1993

Assets		Liabilities and Owner's Equity	
Cash	6000 00	Liabilities	
Equipment	20000 00	Accounts Payable	9000 00
		Owner's Equity	
		J. Hill, Capital	17000 00
Total	26000 00	Total	26000 00

Figure 22.1.   Abbreviated balance sheet

machines purchased but not completely paid for. These amounts owed are called "accounts payable." They are liabilities. The owner of the company is James Hill. His capital account shows his investment in the business.

The fact that assets equal liabilities plus owner's equity is not an accident. Assets stand for the things that a company owns. Liabilities and owner's equity stand for the one who owns them. They are, therefore, different ways of looking at the same thing. This basic fact is expressed in the accounting equation.

$$\text{Assets} = \text{Liabilities} + \text{Owner's Equity}$$

If you know two of these three amounts, you can calculate the third.

DEMONSTRATION EXAMPLE

Company XYZ has assets of $205,700. Liabilities total $127,800. Find the owner's equity amount.

Assets	=	Liabilities	+	Owner's Equity
205,700	=	127,800	+	_____

To find owner's equity, you must subtract: $205,700 - 127,800 = 77,900$.

Owner's equity is $77,900.

EXERCISE 1: ASSETS, LIABILITIES, OWNER'S EQUITY

▶ For each of the following, find the missing amount.

	Assets	=	Liabilities	+	Owner's Equity
1.	$67,900		$45,300		_____
2.	_____		$327,600		$496,500
3.	$761,400		_____		$206,100
4.	$952,400		$682,900		_____
5.	$204,700		$138,200		_____
6.	$1,467,200		_____		$387,200
7.	_____		$894,200		$704,900
8.	_____		$510,638		$307,100
9.	$80,200		$78,600		_____
10.	$2,674,900		_____		$1,083,000
11.	$612,000		$517,400		_____
12.	$198,400		_____		$99,100

The balance sheet contains subcategories to each of the three main areas discussed thus far. Accounts receivable is an asset found frequently on balance sheets. Accounts receivable are amounts that are owed to a company for sales or services sold on credit. These are considered assets because the sale has been made and the company is confident that the customer will pay. A balance sheet for Quick Copy Center one month after it opened is shown in Figure 22.2. There are several accounts receivable and accounts payable as well as a net income amount. This account shows the amount earned by the company during its first month of business.

Quick Copy Center
Balance Sheet
May 31, 1993

Assets		Liabilities and Owner's Equity	
Cash	7400 00	Liabilities	
Accounts Receivable		Accounts Payable	
J. Gomez	1500 00	QX Copy Co.	11900 00
W. O'Keefe	1400 00 2900 00	ABC Machines	2700 00
Equipment	25500 00	Total Liabilities	14600 00
		Owner's Equity	
		J. Hill, Capital	17800 00
		Net Income	3400 00
		Total Owner's Equity	21200 00
Total	35800 00	Total	35800 00

Figure 22.2   Sample balance sheet

EXERCISE 2: COMPLETING A BALANCE SHEET

▶ Complete the following balance sheet. Be sure that the accounting equation is in balance.

Quick Copy Center
Balance Sheet
June 30, 1993

Assets		Liabilities and Owner's Equity	
Cash	6700 00	Liabilities	
Accounts Receivable		Accounts Payable	
J. Gomez	900 00	QX Copy Co.	9600 00
W. O'Keefe	1100 00	ABC Machines	2100 00
Equipment	26200 00	Total Liabilities	
		Owner's Equity	
		J. Hill, Capital	18800 00
		Net Income	4400 00
		Total Owner's Equity	
Total		Total	

Figure 22.3   Practice balance sheet

The simplest accounting form is the T account—so named because it is made in the shape of a capital T. You place debits on the left side of the T and credits on the right side. Increases in asset accounts are placed on the debit (left) side. Decreases are entered on the credit (right) side.

DEMONSTRATION EXAMPLE

Use a T account to show the following cash transactions and the balance. (a) cash receipt, $600; (b) cash payment, $300; (c) cash receipt, $900; (d) cash payment, $500. Notice that the receipts are written on the debit side and the payments on the credit side. Each side is totaled and the balance is written as shown.

	Cash		101
(a)	600	(b)	300
(c)	900	(d)	500
	1,500		800
Debit Balance	700		

Figure 22.4 Sample T account

EXERCISE 3: USING T ACCOUNTS

▶ Using the Ts below, enter the given amounts and find the balance for each of the following cash accounts.

1. Receipt, $900; payment, $300; receipt, $500

2. Receipt, $1,200; receipt, $600; payment, $400; payment, $300

3. Receipt, $350; payment, $75; receipt, $260; receipt, $80

4. Receipt, $980; payment, $320; payment, $245; receipt, $505

5. Receipt, $1,120; payment, $316; payment, $96; payment, $138

6. Receipt, $1,450; receipt, $512; receipt, $102; payment, $1,529

CASH ACCOUNTS

Although T accounts are helpful in understanding how accounting records are kept, it would be inconvenient to use T accounts to maintain actual financial records. These are kept on forms like the one shown in Figure 22.5. A cash account shows increases on the debit side and decreases on the credit side.

EXERCISE 4: COMPLETING CASH ACCOUNTS

▶ Study the sample cash account (Figure 22.5) and then complete the other cash accounts (Figures 22.6 and 22.7) by finding the balance after each entry.

Cash _____ NO. __101__

DATE		EXPLANATION	POST REF.	DEBIT	CREDIT	BALANCE	
						DEBIT	CREDIT
2	1	Balance		6700 00		6700 00	
2	2	Payment Rec'd		925 00		7625 00	
2	3	Purchase			704 00	6921 00	
2	4	Purchase			1196 00	5725 00	

Figure 22.5   Sample cash account

Cash _____ NO. __101__

DATE		EXPLANATION	POST REF.	DEBIT	CREDIT	BALANCE	
						DEBIT	CREDIT
2	10	Balance		6540 00			
2	10	Purchase			716 00		
2	11	Payment Rec'd		1694 00			
2	12	Payment Rec'd		2788 00			

Figure 22.6   Practice cash account 1

EXERCISE 4: COMPLETING CASH ACCOUNTS (continued)

Cash   NO. 101

DATE		EXPLANATION	POST REF.	DEBIT	CREDIT	BALANCE	
						DEBIT	CREDIT
2	15	Balance		8190 00			
2	16	Purchase			2189 00		
2	17	Purchase			534 00		
2	17	Payment Rec'd		916 00			
2	18	Payment Rec'd		474 00			
2	19	Purchase			412 00		

Figure 22.7 Practice cash account 2

EXERCISE 5: ACCOUNTS RECEIVABLE

▶ If a company keeps accounts for a large number of customers, then each customer has a separate account. These are accounts receivable. Increases in what the customer owes are recorded on the debit side. Decreases that occur when the customer makes a payment are recorded on the credit side. A continuous record is kept in the balance column.

The example in Figure 22.8 shows several transactions and the balance after each transaction. Study the example and then complete the other accounts receivable forms (Figures 22.9 and 22.10) by finding the balance after each transaction.

Accts. Rec. / J. Gomez   NO. ___105___

| DATE | | EXPLANATION | POST REF. | DEBIT | CREDIT | BALANCE | |
						DEBIT	CREDIT
2	1	Balance		900 00		900 00	
2	2	Invoice 235		650 00		1550 00	
2	3	Invoice 241		271 00		1821 00	
2	5	Payment Rec'd			500 00	1321 00	

Figure 22.8   Sample accounts receivable form

Accts. Rec. / W. O'Keefe   NO. ___106___

| DATE | | EXPLANATION | POST REF. | DEBIT | CREDIT | BALANCE | |
						DEBIT	CREDIT
2	1	Balance		1100 00			
2	3	Invoice 249		307 00			
2	4	Payment Rec'd			450 00		
2	6	Invoice 260		84 00			

Figure 22.9   Practice accounts receivable form 1

Accts. Rec. / H. Johnson   NO. 107

DATE		EXPLANATION	POST REF.	DEBIT	CREDIT	BALANCE	
						DEBIT	CREDIT
2	1	Invoice 227		19600			
2	3	Invoice 250		27300			
2	5	Invoice 256		8100			
2	7	Payment Rec'd			20000		

Figure 22.10   Practice accounts receivable form 2

EXERCISE 6: ACCOUNTS PAYABLE

▶ Accounts payable stand for payments that the company must make. For accounts payable, increases appear on the credit side and decreases on the debit side.

Study the sample in Figure 22.11 and then complete the accounts payable forms in Figures 22.12 and 22.13.

Accts. Pay. / QX Copy Co.   NO. _201_

DATE		EXPLANATION	POST REF.	DEBIT	CREDIT	BALANCE DEBIT	BALANCE CREDIT
2	1	Balance			9600 00		9600 00
2	2	Purchase			907 00		10507 00
2	3	Payment Rec'd		1200 00			9307 00

Figure 22.11 Sample accounts payable form

Accts. Pay. / ABC Machines   NO. _202_

DATE		EXPLANATION	POST REF.	DEBIT	CREDIT	BALANCE DEBIT	BALANCE CREDIT
2	1	Balance			2100 00		
2	2	Payment		360 00			
2	3	Purchase			479 00		
2	4	Purchase			173 00		

Figure 22.12 Practice accounts payable form 1

Accts. Pay. / Paper Products Inc.   NO. 203

DATE		EXPLANATION	POST REF.	DEBIT	CREDIT	BALANCE	
						DEBIT	CREDIT
2	1	Purchase			825 00		
2	3	Purchase			1293 00		
2	5	Purchase			92 00		
2	7	Payment		750 00			
2	8	Purchase			152 00		

Figure 22.13   Practice accounts payable form 2

Lesson 22
APPLY YOUR SKILLS

▶ Find the balance after each transaction for the following accounts (Figures 22.14 to 22.16).

1. Cash _____ NO. 101

DATE		EXPLANATION	POST REF.	DEBIT	CREDIT	BALANCE	
						DEBIT	CREDIT
6	1	Balance		120000			
6	2	Purchase			26500		
6	3	Purchase			41900		
6	4	Payment Rec'd		70400			

Figure 22.14   Cash account

2. Accts. Rec. / Jane Bruel _____ NO. 103

DATE		EXPLANATION	POST REF.	DEBIT	CREDIT	BALANCE	
						DEBIT	CREDIT
6	1	Balance		53400			
6	2	Invoice 1106		3700			
6	3	Invoice 1119		10500			
6	4	Payment Rec'd			75000		

Figure 22.15   Accounts receivable form

Name _____   254 • Lesson 22

APPLY YOUR SKILLS (continued)

3. <u>Accts. Pay. / Furniture Barn</u>   NO. <u>202</u>

DATE		EXPLANATION	POST REF.	DEBIT	CREDIT	BALANCE	
						DEBIT	CREDIT
6	1	Purchase			79500		
6	2	Purchase			134600		
6	5	Payment		68000			
6	7	Purchase			12700		
6	8	Payment		49000			
6	10	Purchase			27300		

Figure 22.16   Accounts payable form

CHECK YOUR PROGRESS

▶ Find the balance after each transaction for the following accounts (Figures 22.17 to 22.19).

1. **Cash**   NO. **101**

DATE		EXPLANATION	POST REF.	DEBIT	CREDIT	BALANCE	
						DEBIT	CREDIT
9	1	Opening Entry		5300 00			
9	2	Purchase			784 00		
9	3	Purchase			1647 00		
9	5	Payment Rec'd		1297 00			

Figure 22.17 Cash account

2. **Accts. Rec. / R. Tetrac**   NO. **103**

DATE		EXPLANATION	POST REF.	DEBIT	CREDIT	BALANCE	
						DEBIT	CREDIT
9	1	Invoice 501		763 00			
9	2	Invoice 529		296 00			
9	4	Payment Rec'd			420 00		

Figure 22.18 Accounts receivable form

Lesson 22
MASTERY CHECKPOINT

▶ Use the information given and your knowledge of the accounting equation to complete the balance sheet.

Westside Skating Rink
Balance Sheet
June 30, 1993

Assets			Liabilities and Owner's Equity		
Cash		5290 00	Liabilities		
Accts. Rec.			Accts. Payable		
Able Sports Club	960 00		ALL-Sport Inc.	5260 00	
City Comm. Coll.	536 00		KT Electric Co.	1290 00	
Equipment		9470 00	Total Liabilities		
			Owner's Equity		
			R. Ortiz, Capital		
			Net Income	2600 00	
Total			Total Owner's Equity		

Figure 22.19   Balance sheet for Mastery Checkpoint

THE POSTCLOSING
TRIAL BALANCE

OBJECTIVES

After completing this lesson, you will be able to:

- Identify asset, liability, and owner's equity.
- Prepare a postclosing trial balance.

ASSETS, LIABILITY, OWNER'S EQUITY

Accountants use a variety of forms and procedures to prepare financial statements. One of these forms is the postclosing trial balance. To prepare this form, the accountant calculates the balance of a number of different accounts and then writes these balances on a separate form. The total debits and credits are calculated. This is the first step in the preparation of the balance sheet. You will learn the other steps in accounting courses.

The form in Figure 23.1 is the postclosing trial balance for The Fitness Center, an exercise club. Notice that the asset, liability, and owner's equity accounts are contained on the form. But on this form they are all listed vertically. As you saw in the previous lesson, the asset accounts have a debit balance; the liability and owner's equity accounts have a credit balance. The two sides of the accounting equation must balance. That is, assets equal liabilities plus owner's equity.

The Fitness Center
Postclosing Trial Balance
June 30, 1993

ACCT. NO.	ACCOUNT NAME	DEBIT	CREDIT
101	Cash	12700 00	
102	Accounts Receivable	2400 00	
111	Exercise Equipment	17300 00	
112	Furniture	1800 00	
201	Accounts Payable		14500 00
301	Joan Li, Capital		19700 00

Figure 23.1   Sample postclosing trial balance

EXERCISE 1: POSTCLOSING TRIAL BALANCE

▶ Check to see that the accounting equation is in balance for the postclosing trial balance (Figure 23.2).

The Fitness Center
Postclosing Trial Balance
July 31, 1993

ACCT. NO.	ACCOUNT NAME	DEBIT	CREDIT
101	Cash	10800 00	
102	Accounts Receivable	3400 00	
111	Exercise Equipment	18900 00	
112	Furniture	2000 00	
201	Accounts Payable		12500 00
301	Joan Li, Capital		22600 00

Figure 23.2   Postclosing trial balance

Name _____   262 • Lesson 23

▶ Find the amount for the liabilities account that will balance the postclosing trial balance (Figure 23.3).

The Fitness Center
Postclosing Trial Balance
August 31, 1993

ACCT. NO.	ACCOUNT NAME	DEBIT	CREDIT
101	Cash	11400 00	
102	Accounts Receivable	2900 00	
111	Exercise Equipment	27600 00	
112	Furniture	1800 00	
201	Accounts Payable		
301	Joan Li, Capital		22400 00

Figure 23.3   Postclosing trial balance

Name _____

▶ Find the amount for the owner's equity account that will balance the postclosing trial balance (Figure 23.4).

The Fitness Center
Postclosing Trial Balance
September 31, 1993

ACCT. NO.	ACCOUNT NAME	DEBIT	CREDIT
101	Cash	1220 00	
102	Accounts Receivable	270 00	
111	Exercise Equipment	3140 00	
112	Furniture	160 00	
201	Accounts Payable		2470 00
301	Joan Li, Capital		

Figure 23.4   Postclosing trial balance

Lesson 23
APPLY YOUR SKILLS

▶ Take the balance amount from the six accounts below (Figures 23.5–23.10) and write it on the line for that account on the postclosing trial balance (Figure 23.11). Then check to see that the accounting equation is in balance for the postclosing trial balance.

Cash   NO. __101__

DATE	EXPLANATION	POST REF.	DEBIT	CREDIT	BALANCE	
					DEBIT	CREDIT
10 31	Balance				13600 00	

Figure 23.5   Balance 1

Accounts Receivable / W. Belstock   NO. __102__

DATE	EXPLANATION	POST REF.	DEBIT	CREDIT	BALANCE	
					DEBIT	CREDIT
10 31	Balance				1400 00	

Figure 23.6   Balance 2

Exercise Equipment   NO. __111__

DATE	EXPLANATION	POST REF.	DEBIT	CREDIT	BALANCE	
					DEBIT	CREDIT
10 31	Balance				29800 00	

Figure 23.7   Balance 3

Furniture _____ NO. 112

DATE	EXPLANATION	POST REF.	DEBIT	CREDIT	BALANCE	
					DEBIT	CREDIT
10 31	Balance				1400 00	

Figure 23.8   Balance 4

Accounts Payable _____ NO. 201

DATE	EXPLANATION	POST REF.	DEBIT	CREDIT	BALANCE	
					DEBIT	CREDIT
10 31	Balance					22600 00

Figure 23.9   Balance 5

Joan Li, Capital _____ NO. 301

DATE	EXPLANATION	POST REF.	DEBIT	CREDIT	BALANCE	
					DEBIT	CREDIT
10 31	Balance					23600 00

Figure 23.10   Balance 6

APPLY YOUR SKILLS (continued)

The Fitness Center
Postclosing Trial Balance
October 31, 1993

ACCT. NO.	ACCOUNT NAME	DEBIT	CREDIT
101	Cash		
102	Accounts Receivable		
111	Exercise Equipment		
112	Furniture		
201	Accounts Payable		
301	Joan Li, Capital		

Figure 23.11   Postclosing trial balance

CHECK YOUR PROGRESS

▶ Review your knowledge of the accounting rules studied. Complete each statement by filling in the blank or circling the correct word.

1. Write the accounting equation. _____

2. Debits are written on the (right, left) column on an accounting form.

3. Asset accounts generally have a (debit, credit) balance.

4. Accounts payable is an (asset, liability, owner's equity) account.

5. Assets are _____

Lesson 23
MASTERY CHECKPOINT

▶ Use the balance amounts from the six accounts below (Figures 23.12 to 23.17) to prepare a postclosing trial balance (Figure 23.18). Write the names of the accounts and then the amounts on the postclosing trial balance form. Then check to see that the accounting equation is in balance.

Cash   NO. __101__

DATE	EXPLANATION	POST REF.	DEBIT	CREDIT	BALANCE	
					DEBIT	CREDIT
11 30	Balance				11900 00	

Figure 23.12   Balance 1

Accounts Receivable / W. Belstock   NO. __102__

DATE	EXPLANATION	POST REF.	DEBIT	CREDIT	BALANCE	
					DEBIT	CREDIT
11 30	Balance				1700 00	

Figure 23.13   Balance 2

Exercise Equipment   NO. __111__

DATE	EXPLANATION	POST REF.	DEBIT	CREDIT	BALANCE	
					DEBIT	CREDIT
11 30	Balance				34800 00	

Figure 23.14   Balance 3

Furniture   NO. 112

DATE	EXPLANATION	POST REF.	DEBIT	CREDIT	BALANCE	
					DEBIT	CREDIT
11 30	Balance				1600 00	

Figure 23.15　Balance 4

Accounts Payable   NO. 201

DATE	EXPLANATION	POST REF.	DEBIT	CREDIT	BALANCE	
					DEBIT	CREDIT
11 30	Balance					26500 00

Figure 23.16　Balance 5

Joan Li, Capital   NO. 301

DATE	EXPLANATION	POST REF.	DEBIT	CREDIT	BALANCE	
					DEBIT	CREDIT
11 30	Balance					23500 00

Figure 23.17　Balance 6

The Fitness Center
Postclosing Trial Balance
November 30, 1993

ACCT. NO.	ACCOUNT NAME	DEBIT	CREDIT

Figure 23.18 Postclosing trial balance

Name _____

Index